The Ebola Virus

© 2007 Thomson Gale, a part of The Thomson Corporation.

Thomson and Star Logo are trademarks and Gale and Lucent Books are registered trademarks used herein under license.

For more information, contact
Lucent Books
27500 Drake Rd.
Farmington Hills, MI 48331-3535
Or you can visit our Internet site at http://www.gale.com

LIBRARY OF CONGRESS CATALOGING-IN-PUBLICATION DATA

Hirschmann, Kris, 1967-
    The ebola virus / by Kris Hirschmann.
        p. cm. — (Diseases and disorders series)
    Includes bibliographical references and index.
    Contents: Death in Africa—The science of Ebola—Ebola reappears—
Containing Ebola—Staying one step ahead.
    ISBN 1-59018-672-9 (hardcover : alk. paper)
    1. Ebola virus disease—Juvenile literature. I. Title. II. Series: Diseases and
disorders series.
RC140.5.H57 2007
616.9'2—dc22
                                                              2006017276

Printed in the United States

Table of Contents

"The Most Difficult Puzzles Ever Devised"

Charles Best, one of the pioneers in the search for a cure for diabetes, once explained what it is about medical research that intrigued him so. "It's not just the gratification of knowing one is helping people," he confided, "although that probably is a more heroic and selfless motivation. Those feelings may enter in, but truly, what I find best is the feeling of going toe to toe with nature, of trying to solve the most difficult puzzles ever devised. The answers are there somewhere, those keys that will solve the puzzle and make the patient well. But how will those keys be found?"

Since the dawn of civilization, nothing has so puzzled people— and often frightened them, as well—as the onset of illness in a body or mind that had seemed healthy before. A seizure, the inability of a heart to pump, the sudden deterioration of muscle tone in a small child—being unable to reverse such conditions or even to understand why they occur was unspeakably frustrating to healers. Even before there were names for such conditions, even before they were understood at all, each was a reminder of how complex the human body was, and how vulnerable.

While our grappling with understanding diseases has been frustrating at times, it has also provided some of humankind's most heroic accomplishments. Alexander Fleming's accidental discovery in 1928 of a mold that could be turned into penicillin has resulted in the saving of untold millions of lives. The isolation of the enzyme insulin has reversed what was once a death sentence for anyone with diabetes. There have been great strides in combating conditions for which there is not yet a cure, too. Medicines can help AIDS patients live longer, diagnostic tools such as mammography and ultrasounds can help doctors find tumors while they are treatable, and laser surgery techniques have made the most intricate, minute operations routine.

This "toe-to-toe" competition with diseases and disorders is even more remarkable when seen in a historical continuum. An astonishing amount of progress has been made in a very short time. Just two hundred years ago, the existence of germs as a cause of some diseases was unknown. In fact, it was less than 150 years ago that a British surgeon named Joseph Lister had difficulty persuading his fellow doctors that washing their hands before delivering a baby might increase the chances of a healthy delivery (especially if they had just attended to a diseased patient)!

Each book in Lucent's Diseases and Disorders series explores a disease or disorder and the knowledge that has been accumulated (or discarded) by doctors through the years. Each book also examines the tools used for pinpointing a diagnosis, as well as the various means that are used to treat or cure a disease. Finally, new ideas are presented—techniques or medicines that may be on the horizon.

Frustration and disappointment are still part of medicine, for not every disease or condition can be cured or prevented. But the limitations of knowledge are being pushed outward constantly; the "most difficult puzzles ever devised" are finding challengers every day.

Emerging Diseases

The mid-1900s were a sunny time in the world medical community. Thanks to antibiotics, deadly diseases such as typhoid fever and tuberculosis were suddenly easy to cure. A vaccine was developed for smallpox, an illness that killed several million people per year during the first half of the century. Vaccines also became available for illnesses such as polio and diphtheria, which once struck hundreds of thousands of children each year. Death from infectious diseases became less and less common in developed nations as inoculation programs were established, and medical organizations everywhere declared that humankind was winning the war on microbes.

This view turned out to be much too optimistic, however. Although humans have conquered some old microbial enemies, many new ones have appeared to take their place. The list of diseases discovered in the past few decades includes Legionnaires' disease, Lyme disease, hantavirus pulmonary syndrome, severe acute respiratory syndrome (SARS), and, of course, acquired immunodeficiency syndrome (AIDS), all of which are unpleasant at best and deadly at worst. As a group, these syndromes are called emerging diseases.

All emerging diseases are worrisome. But few are as frightening as two African illnesses: Ebola hemorrhagic fever and its nearly identical relative, Marburg hemorrhagic fever. These viral diseases appear without warning, bring an astonishingly fast and gruesome death to their human victims, and then go back into hiding. They cannot be prevented, and they cannot

A scientist takes a blood sample from a young resident of Zaire, Africa, during the 1975 outbreak of the deadly Ebola virus.

be cured. Of the two viruses, Ebola is fractionally worse; it kills up to 90 percent of the people it infects. Marburg was once thought to be gentler, killing only 25 percent of its victims. In two recent epidemics that affected hundreds of people, however, eight out of every ten Marburg patients died.

Marburg and Ebola were discovered in 1967 and 1976, respectively. Since then, they have caused multiple outbreaks and thousands of human deaths in Africa. Because Ebola has done most of this damage, it is much better known than Marburg, and it is feared with a manic intensity by potential victims and the medical community alike. Until the disease can be prevented, treated, or reliably contained, it will continue to inspire fear in everyone it affects.

CHAPTER ONE

Death in Africa

Equatorial Africa is dominated by the Congo River basin. This massive rain forest region stretches about 1,350 miles (2,170km) through the center of the continent and covers an area equal to about half of the continental United States. The basin is hot and humid, and it teems with biting and stinging creatures. It is so densely vegetated that travel is usually difficult and in some places impossible. Isolated villages and a few larger cities dot the landscape, but tourists and other outsiders seldom visit this wild and generally unwelcoming place. In fact, a few decades ago, recalls one virologist, the Congo River basin was "as remote as any on the face of the planet. Few people outside of the region had any idea of what was to be found there."[1]

In 1976, however, this out-of-the-way area became the focus of international attention. The cause of the uproar was a mysterious disease that erupted simultaneously in the rain forest nation of Zaire (now known as the Democratic Republic of the Congo) and in neighboring Sudan. The unknown illness developed quickly, it had horrifying symptoms, and it was clearly infectious. Killing up to 90 percent of its victims, it was also one of the deadliest diseases ever to strike humankind. Although no one knew it at the time, the virus now known as Ebola was making its first appearance.

Ebola Appears

The first outbreak began quietly in the town of Nzara. This community of about twenty thousand people is located in southern Sudan, just above the Zairian border. In 1976 most Nzara residents were fieldworkers. A few lucky men avoided this difficult lifestyle by taking jobs at the local cotton factory. With more than 450 workers, the factory was by far the town's largest employer.

One of the cotton factory's employees is remembered today as YuG. YuG was a strong, healthy man who seldom felt sick. But on June 27, 1976, he woke up with a severe headache. The pain soon became so intense that YuG feared he might vomit. The sick man next developed a high fever and a sore throat. The inside of his mouth became bone dry and cracked. YuG needed water, but swallowing was agony, so he drank very little. His body started to show signs of dehydration. At the same time, YuG was wracked by increasingly painful muscle spasms that struck his back, legs, chest, and neck.

By June 30 YuG was so ill that he could only lie, groaning, on his bed. Alarmed relatives sent him to the local hospital, a

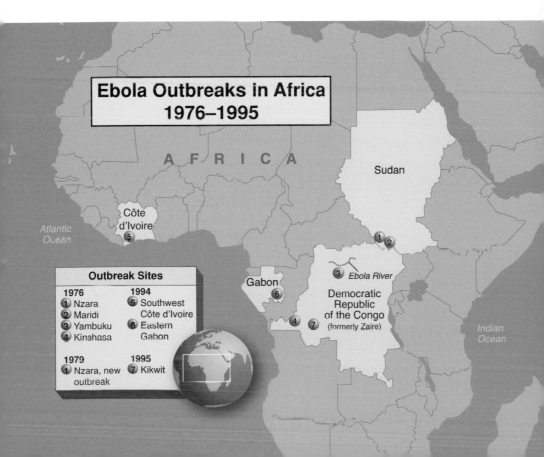

Ebola Outbreaks in Africa 1976–1995

AFRICA

Sudan

Côte d'Ivoire
5

Atlantic Ocean

1 2

3 Ebola River

Gabon
6

Outbreak Sites

1976	1994
1 Nzara	5 Southwest Côte d'Ivoire
2 Maridi	6 Eastern Gabon
3 Yambuku	
4 Kinshasa	

1979	1995
1 Nzara, new outbreak	7 Kikwit

Democratic Republic of the Congo (formerly Zaire)

Indian Ocean

Viral Hemorrhagic Fevers

Ebola and Marburg are both classified as viral hemorrhagic fevers (VHFs). There are many well-known VHFs in addition to Ebola and Marburg.

Yellow fever is probably the best-known VHF. This disease has been devastating human populations for centuries. Although an effective vaccine exists, yellow fever still causes two hundred thousand illnesses and thirty thousand deaths per year (a 15 percent mortality rate) among unvaccinated populations.

Less common but deadlier than yellow fever is Crimean-Congo hemorrhagic fever (CCHF). This tick-borne illness has erupted several times in central Asia, Turkey, and Zaire since its discovery in 1944. About 30 percent of those who contract CCHF die. Another VHF called Machupo hemorrhagic fever has the same kill rate, bringing death to as many as 30 percent of its human victims. Also known as Bolivian hemorrhagic fever, this disease came to light in 1959 and is native to Bolivia.

Two milder VHFs are Lassa fever and dengue hemorrhagic fever. Lassa fever appeared in 1969 in Nigeria but now occurs throughout West Africa. It strikes hundreds of thousands of people each year and kills about five thousand. Dengue hemorrhagic fever, which has been known since the 1780s, is common throughout the tropics. Transmitted to humans through mosquito bites, this disease is rarely fatal.

primitive facility that was run by one doctor and one nurse. The medical professionals had no idea what was wrong with YuG. They did everything they could think of to help the distressed man, but nothing seemed to work. The patient got sicker and sicker as the days passed. He developed stomach cramps, bloody diarrhea, and vomiting. He also started to bleed heavily from his nose and mouth. The flesh seemed to melt from his bones as the disease progressed. YuG finally died on July 6, just ten days after his first symptoms had appeared.

The Disease Spreads

Less than a week later, the illness struck again. On July 12 another cotton factory worker, known as Bz, showed up at the Nzara hospital with symptoms identical to those of YuG. But unlike YuG, who had arrived at the hospital soon after he became sick, Bz was deathly ill by the time he sought help. He could barely move, and he was bleeding from his nose and mouth. His diarrhea and vomit were also bloody. As they had done with YuG, the medical staff tried their best to help Bz, but they could not give the patient any relief. Bz died on July 14, just two days after he was admitted to the hospital.

By this time the unknown illness was cropping up among the families of the deceased. First YuG's brother came down with the disease, then Bz's wife. Both of these people had nursed their sick relatives before bringing them to the hospital. Now patients themselves, they showed all of the horrific symptoms the Nzara staff were coming to dread. Bz's wife declined quickly and soon died. YuG's brother was luckier. He

In 1976, the first Sudanese victims of the Ebola virus were laid to rest in this graveyard.

fought the disease for weeks but eventually recovered, becoming the first-known survivor of the epidemic.

At this point it seemed that the outbreak might be dying down. But unknown to anyone, including himself, a third factory worker, known as PG, was carrying the same disease that had killed his coworkers. PG was a fun-loving bachelor with girlfriends and contacts all over town, and he spent time with many people before his symptoms became severe. He finally got sick enough to seek medical help on July 18, and he died on July 27. However, his illness did not die with him. Several of PG's girlfriends came down with the disease. The girlfriends were tended by their family members, many of whom also became sick. These new cases then passed the deadly illness to others. The outbreak worsened as the disease claimed victims in an ever-widening circle.

Besides his girlfriends, PG had also infected at least one casual acquaintance before entering the hospital. Hoping for superior care, the friend traveled to Maridi, a larger town about 80 miles (129km) east of Nzara. He spent ten days in Maridi's hospital before dying. During this time, the friend transmitted his illness to hospital workers, who then gave it to other patients. It was now mid-August, and the seeds of a full-blown epidemic had been planted.

Outbreak in Zaire

Meanwhile, about 500 miles (805km) to the southwest, life was going on as usual in the Zairian town of Yambuku. In 1976 the town's largest and best-known establishment was the Yambuku Mission Hospital, a clinic run by several Belgian nuns. Local people traveled to the clinic from scattered villages to receive first aid for injuries, give birth to babies, and get injections for the many all-too-common illnesses that plagued the region. On a typical day, dozens of people lined up at the clinic's door seeking treatment.

The first sign of trouble appeared on August 26, when mission worker Mabalo Lokela woke up feeling ill. Lokela thought he had malaria, so he asked the nun on duty to give him an antimalaria injection. The nun agreed with Lokela's diagnosis.

Simultaneous but Separate

Although Ebola broke out in two separate places, the epidemics were initially thought to be related. Scientists believed an infected person had carried the disease between Sudan and Zaire, thereby sparking a second outbreak. After personally making the land journey from Yambuku to Nzara, however, virologist Joseph B. McCormick came to question this view. He says about his difficult journey:

The road we took was little more than a path. . . . The whole northern area [of Zaire] had been neglected, and none of the roads and bridges were maintained. We almost never caught sight of another vehicle. Why would anyone in his right mind want to drive up here, and where in the world would they be going?

I began to harbor serious doubts about whether there could be a connection between the two outbreaks of Ebola. In this part of the world, if anyone needs to travel, they either walk or ride a bicycle; their horizons are generally limited by the distances they can cover in a day. With travel between Zaire and the Sudan so difficult, it was unlikely that many people would have been in a position to transmit the disease from one location to the other. . . . It would have been an impossible walk or bike ride for an infected person.

Laboratory studies later proved McCormick correct. The Zaire and Sudan epidemics, though simultaneous, had been caused by two distinct strains of Ebola.

Joseph B. McCormick and Susan Fisher-Hoch, *Level 4: Virus Hunters of the CDC.* Atlanta: Turner, 1996, p. 59.

She picked up a syringe that had already been used several times that morning, filled it with the drug, and administered the injection. She rinsed the needle with water and set the syringe back on its tray, ready to be used on the next patient. Then she sent Lokela home to get some rest.

Lokela felt much better after his injection. By September 1, however, he was feeling sick again. He developed a high fever and a terrible headache, and he passed bloody stools. His stomach churned with cramps and he could not stop vomiting. Lokela was admitted to the clinic, where he was tended by his wife, Sophie Mbunzu. Mbunzu and the nuns watched with horror as Lokela's illness progressed. Like the hospital staff in Nzara, they tried everything they could think of to break the disease's deadly grip, but nothing worked. Lokela became increasingly sicker until he died on September 9.

Back at home, a stunned Mbunzu prepared her husband's body for burial. In accordance with local custom, she and Lokela's other female relatives cleaned the corpse with their bare hands. They hugged and kissed the body as they worked. With each hug, they transferred a little bit of Lokela's sickness

When caregivers failed to sterilize syringes at Sudan's Maridi Hospital (pictured) and Zaire's Yambuku Mission Hospital, the sites became breeding grounds for Ebola.

onto their own skin. With each kiss, they took the disease into their mouths.

From a Trickle to a Flow

Mbunzu fell ill soon after her husband's death, as did Lokela's mother and sister. Unrelated people started to get sick as well. The day after Lokela died, the Yambuku nuns discovered six new cases of what they were now calling "the fever." And according to the clinic's patients, in the surrounding villages were many more sufferers who had not yet visited the mission.

Over the next few days the trickle of desperately ill people arriving at the clinic turned into a flow. The nuns had no idea what was causing the illness, but they guessed it might be a severe form of malaria, typhoid, or some other common disease. Even though the usual drugs did not seem to do any good, the nuns continued to administer quinine, vitamins, and everything else in their meager medical arsenal. All of these substances were given by injection. After each injection, a nun rinsed the needle, then used the contaminated syringe to inject another patient. The epidemic spread silently as the sisters administered their deadly care.

It took less than a week for the situation to erupt. Virtually overnight, people in fifty-five villages near Yambuku came down with the fever. Many of these people had visited the mission for injections. Others had tended sick family members or helped to bury deceased friends or relatives. All of the victims had headaches, fevers, body pains, and the rest of the symptoms first seen in Mabalo Lokela. They vomited, they bled—and they died in droves. The mysterious disease killed practically everyone it touched. Terrified that they would be next, healthy villagers quarantined their sick neighbors and blocked the roads to prevent strangers from passing through. But no matter what people did to protect themselves, every day brought new cases of the fever and new deaths.

Things were just as bad back at the mission. By mid-September the clinic's beds were full of dead and dying people. Eleven of the seventeen mission workers, including one of the nuns, had taken ill. The remaining staff members were exhausted, overwhelmed, and frightened. They decided to use the mission's radio—their only point of contact with the outside world—to call for more experienced help.

Word Gets Out

Immediately after the sisters placed their call, Dr. Ngoï, a medical official, visited Yambuku Mission Hospital. He examined the patients and spoke to the nuns at length. When he had gathered as much information as possible, he wrote everything down and sent the report to his superiors. Entitled "An Inquiry into the Alarming Cases in the Collectivity of Yandongi, in the Zone of Bumba, 15–17 September, 1976," this report was the first official document to describe the Yambuku epidemic.

News of the outbreak spread through official channels over the next two weeks. High-ranking Zairian officials were among the first to learn of Yambuku's plight, but they did nothing about it. Zaire itself did not have the resources to deal with the problem, and officials were reluctant to involve the Western world. Still, the situation in Yambuku was too alarming to remain a secret forever. The epidemic came to the attention of international health organizations in early October; news of the Sudan outbreak arrived a little later. By this time hundreds of people had died in both places, including a nun who had been examined by Dr. Ngoï. Two other nuns had fallen ill and had been taken to a hospital in the Zairian capital city of Kinshasa, where officials feared they would spawn a new outbreak. Realizing that the situation had become explosive, the Zairian and Sudanese governments granted permission for Western medical teams to visit the epidemic sites.

The teams mobilized quickly and arrived within days in both Nzara and Yambuku to begin their investigations. They were immediately greeted by a series of gruesome discoveries. At one Zairian hospital, for instance, officials went to visit a sick husband and wife but found both people dead. In the words of physician Frank Ryan:

Everywhere in the small cubicle was the pervasive evidence of the suffering this couple had gone through. The

In 1976, a group of western medical professionals brought in to investigate the Ebola epidemic poses for a photo in Yambuku, Zaire.

room was disorganized and clearly had not been cleaned since their arrival. There was a nauseating stench of death. [The woman] was lying on a bed wearing . . . soiled clothes . . . There was no linen on the bed. Bloody tracks ran from her mouth, nose, eyes, and even her ears. Her husband was half reclining in a chair, his head thrown back. . . . Once again there was evidence of bleeding from his mouth, nose, and eyes, and soiling of the chair from his excretions.[2]

This type of scene soon became familiar to the investigators. Wearing protective suits, the medical teams visited filthy, disease-ridden huts and hospital wards. They drew blood sample after blood sample from dying people, and they clipped tissue samples from corpses. The samples were packed in dry ice and shipped off to infectious disease laboratories in England and Belgium for analysis.

A Shocking Discovery

By October 10, samples from the Zaire outbreak had made their way not only to Europe but also to the Centers for Disease

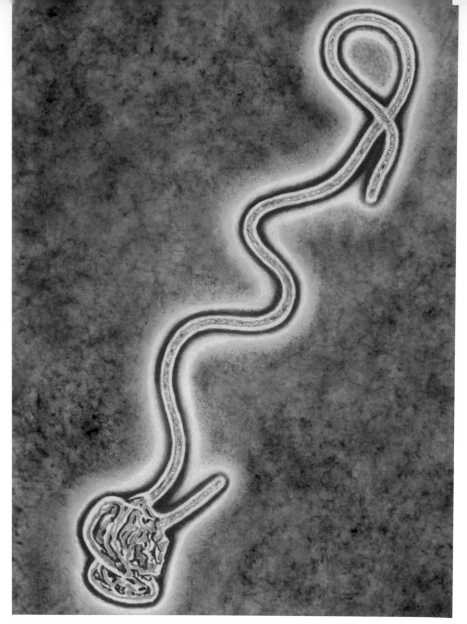

In 1976, upon examination by the Centers for Disease Control (CDC), the deadly Ebola virus (pictured) was determined to be a new disease.

Control and Prevention (CDC) in Atlanta, Georgia. Some of the test tubes holding the samples broke along the way. The virologists who received the dripping packages pulled on latex gloves to retrieve the contents, but they took no other precautions.

One of these virologists was Patricia Webb. A scientist who worked in the CDC's Special Pathogens Branch, Webb was responsible for growing cultures from the African specimens. To do this, she introduced diseased material into flasks containing live monkey cells. Within two or three days the previously healthy monkey cells were curling, changing color, and pulling away from each other. These changes were signs that a disease-causing virus was at work.

Webb called Fred Murphy, the CDC's chief of viral pathology, and told him about her results. Murphy immediately prepared a sample of the sick monkey cells for viewing under an electron microscope. Wearing a surgical gown, mask, and gloves, Murphy slid the sample into the microscope, then flipped on the instrument's viewing screen. What he saw stunned him. "Virtually immediately I saw long curled filaments, absolutely unique among all the viruses. It looked exactly like Marburg. . . . The hairs stood up on my neck,"[3] he remembers. Murphy backed away from the microscope and grabbed a bottle of bleach. He scrubbed every surface of the laboratory to destroy any virus he might have left behind. Then he returned to the microscope and snapped a now-famous picture of the ropelike microbe on the screen.

Murphy was shaken by his discovery, and with good reason. Marburg hemorrhagic fever (MHF) is contagious, fast-moving, and extremely dangerous. Ever since the disease had been discovered in 1967, virologists had feared a major outbreak. Now it looked like it had happened.

But as it turned out, it had not. Tests soon revealed that the infectious agent was not the Marburg virus but rather a close relative that looked almost the same and that caused identical symptoms. The only real difference between the new disease and MHF, in fact, involved mortality rates. At that time Marburg had killed about 25 percent of its victims, but its new-found cousin was fatal up to 90 percent of the time. It was the medical community's worst nightmare come true. The deadliest virus ever discovered was on the loose, and no one knew how to stop it from spreading.

Stopping the Killer

Yet stop it they must, somehow. Now named Ebola hemorrhagic fever after a river north of Yambuku, the disease was still claiming scores of victims in Sudan and Zaire. So far the epidemics had not spread to any major cities, but if they were not contained soon, they surely would. Officials shuddered at the idea of Ebola erupting in a densely populated area. With a 90 percent mortality rate, the disease might turn a bustling city into a ghost town within a few weeks. It was absolutely critical to prevent the twin Ebola epidemics from getting any worse.

With this goal in mind, containment teams operating under the authority of the World Health Organization (WHO) headed to Africa. Because no one knew how Ebola was transmitted, the teams faced a difficult and potentially deadly task. Team leader Karl Johnson recalls, "We knew we were dealing with something new. We didn't know if the virus could be spread by droplets in the air, somewhat like influenza. . . . It would have been *exceedingly* difficult to contain that virus if it had had any major respiratory component."[4] Still, Johnson, who was then the director of the CDC's Special Pathogens Branch, and his colleagues knew they had to try.

In a 1995 photo, nurses in Zaire change the bed linens in an Ebola isolation ward. Such wards were also set up during the 1976 Ebola outbreak.

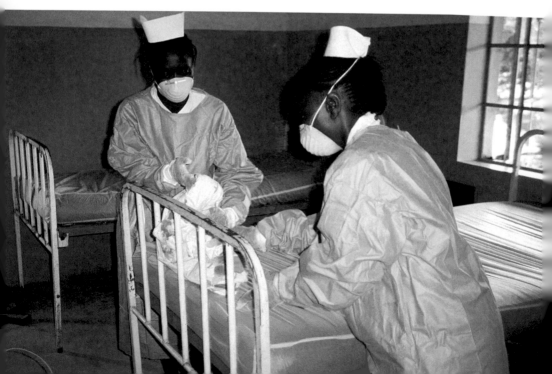

Johnson's team reached Zaire on October 18, and another team arrived in Sudan on October 20. Both teams headed straight for the local hospitals, where they discovered that many doctors, nurses, and medical assistants had already died of Ebola. Others were critically ill, and most of those who remained healthy had fled. But a few cooperative and willing staff members remained. These workers were immediately taught how to avoid spreading bodily fluids from one patient to another or to themselves. This simple step halted Ebola's spread through hospitals, thereby blocking the epidemic's major transmission route.

Isolation of Ebola victims was the next step. Controlled-access hospital wards were established to keep patients from infecting their families and friends. Containment teams also visited local villages and instituted strict quarantines anywhere they found the disease festering. When patients died, officials took charge of the corpses and disposed of them in safe ways. Throughout it all, team members protected themselves by wearing miserably uncomfortable respirators, ankle-length plastic aprons, and surgical gowns. "To those patients, we must have looked like creatures from outer space,"[5] remarks one team member.

Working with Ebola victims was difficult, dangerous, and discouraging, but it got results. The number of new cases started to decline as October rolled into November. Officials who noticed the trend were at first skeptical, then hopeful, then cautiously optimistic. Finally there came a day when all doubt disappeared. Ebola was definitely retreating; global disaster had been averted. Health authorities were thrilled by this news, but they were also shocked by the epidemic's final toll. There had been 284 confirmed cases and 150 deaths in Sudan, a 53 percent fatality rate. In Zaire the fever had sickened 318 people, of whom 280 had died—an incredible 88 percent fatality rate.

On Ebola's Trail

As the Zaire and Sudan epidemics died down, the scientists on site increased their information-gathering efforts. They took hundreds of blood and tissue samples from sick patients and

A nurse working at Ngaliema Hospital (pictured) died of Ebola in 1976. Stored samples of her infected blood have long been invaluable to virologists studying the disease.

corpses. From the few lucky survivors, they took blood serum that they hoped would point the way to an Ebola vaccine or perhaps even to a cure. Each day's samples were processed and packaged at night, then shipped to overseas laboratories. This work was time-consuming and monotonous, but it was vitally important. Scientists needed to preserve virus samples so they could study Ebola once the epidemic disappeared.

In Zaire the blood of a nurse named Mayinga turned out to be one critical sample. Mayinga was working at busy Ngaliema Hospital in Kinshasa when she became ill with Ebola. Although the sick nurse received the full attention of the WHO team, she did not survive her illness. Still, Mayinga's case taught virologists a great deal about the course and handling of Ebola. Even more important than this knowledge was Mayinga's virus-laden blood, which is still preserved today in laboratories around the world. As virologist Joseph B. McCormick of the CDC explains, "The virus that was extracted from her blood would turn out to be a kind of bequest to humanity, since it has been the source of virtually all knowledge we've subsequently obtained about this previously unknown virus and its effects on the human body."[6]

Meanwhile, other pieces of the Ebola puzzle were being gathered in Nzara. Besides collecting human samples, officials in this region were also combing the cotton factory for clues. They collected rats, bats, birds, lizards, insects, and spiders from the infested facility, then shipped their blood and organs away for laboratory analysis. Trapping and packing the samples was a filthy job, and examining them would put lab workers at risk of illness. But if Ebola was lurking somewhere inside these samples, all the effort would be worthwhile. By discovering the virus's hiding place, scientists might be able to guess where Ebola would strike next.

CHAPTER TWO

The Science of Ebola

When Ebola hemorrhagic fever first erupted in 1976, it was terrifying mostly because it was unknown. Scientists had no idea what caused the disease, how it spread, or how to treat it. But this ignorance did not last long. Determined not to be blindsided again, virologists set to work studying Ebola even before the initial outbreaks died down. Over the next three decades the world medical community learned a great deal about Ebola's physical shape, behavior, symptoms, and other aspects of the disease.

"A Tub of Spaghetti"

Disease can be caused by many different infectious agents, including parasites, bacteria, and viruses. In the case of Ebola, the agent is a virus of the scientific family Filoviridae. Ebola and its relative, Marburg, are the only known filoviruses. So far, four distinct strains of Ebola have been discovered. They are named after the places where they first erupted: Ebola-Zaire (1976), Ebola-Sudan (1976), Ebola-Reston (1989), and Ebola-Côte d'Ivoire (1994). Ebola-Zaire and Ebola-Sudan are the best-known members of this deadly family. Ebola-Zaire is by far the most dangerous strain; it kills close to 90 percent of the people it infects. Ebola-Sudan is milder, bringing death to 50 percent of its victims.

Viewed under an electron microscope, all four Ebola strains share a distinctive and immediately identifiable shape. While the virions, or individual particles, of most other virus families are rounded, those of the Filoviridae are long and threadlike. The name *filovirus*, which derives from Latin words meaning "thread virus," was actually chosen because of this feature. Science writer Richard Preston graphically describes filoviruses with these words: "The thread viruses have been compared to strands of tangled rope, to hair, to worms, to snakes. When they appear in a great flooding mess, as they so often do when they have destroyed a victim, they look like a tub of spaghetti that has been dumped on the floor."[7]

Terminal bends are another unique filovirus feature. One end of each Ebola virion is twisted into a loop. As a result, the entire particle resembles a rodeo lasso or, as Preston puts it, "a Cheerio with a long tail."[8] Sometimes a virion ends in several such loops, which are usually called eyebolts or shepherd's crooks.

On a structural level, Ebola consists of genetic information inside a spike-studded protein shell. The genetic information is carried by a single coiled strand of ribonucleic acid (RNA), which acts like a blueprint for the virus's shape, behavior, and

A colored micrograph of a colony of Ebola viruses reveals their resemblance to ropes or snakes.

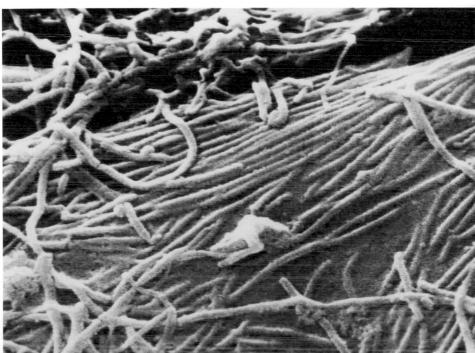

other traits. The protein shell is similar in function to the gelatin capsule of a headache pill, surrounding and protecting the precious material inside. The seven proteins that build the shell have individual functions as well, most of which scientists do not understand.

Ebola Enters the Body

Ebola virions are not considered living creatures. They do not move independently, eat, or breathe, and they cannot multiply on their own. But like all viruses, they can reproduce by hijacking the functions of living cells. The first step in this process is finding and entering a suitable host—and many creatures, including human beings, make excellent targets.

The first human case in an Ebola epidemic is called the index case. Most index cases become ill after they handle or eat infected animals. Because monkey meat is a food staple in many parts of Africa, diseased monkeys are the most common source of Ebola outbreaks. Antelope meat has also been known to transmit the disease. Occasionally the source of an outbreak cannot be traced because the index case either is unknown or does not recall touching or eating any animals recently.

Once a person becomes infected, he or she can pass the disease to other people. Unlike influenza and other airborne viruses, Ebola does not leap readily across open spaces. It is transmitted only by direct contact with bodily fluids such as blood, vomit, mucus, diarrhea, or semen. For this reason, Ebola is most likely to spread to a patient's closest contacts, such as family members or caregivers. Casual contacts usually are not infected.

The most dangerous type of transmission occurs when a person is exposed to a contaminated instrument. Contamination takes place when a hypodermic needle, a knife, or another instrument is used to treat an Ebola patient. During the treatment, the instrument picks up a load of virus. If the unsterilized instrument is used on another person, it dumps part of its deadly load into the new patient's bloodstream. In such a case, infection is certain, fast, and deadly. During the Zaire epidemic of 1976, 100 percent of those infected by injection lost their lives.

A Dangerous Job

Modern scientists know how dangerous Ebola is, and they take every imaginable precaution when working with it. But no matter how careful they are, mistakes are always possible. Several laboratory workers have become Ebola victims after little accidents turned into big problems.

One lab incident occurred in 1976, soon after Ebola was discovered. Virologist Geoff Platt was conducting experiments with the virus at England's Porton Down research facility. Attempting to inject a squirming rodent one Friday afternoon, Platt missed the mark and jabbed his own thumb instead. He showed the first symptoms of Ebola the following Tuesday and deteriorated rapidly thereafter. Platt spent two weeks in intensive care, hovering near death for much of that time, but he eventually recovered from the incident.

Another lab exposure took place in 2004 at the Vektor Research Institute in Russia. On May 5, scientist Antonina Presnyakova was taking blood from Ebola-infected guinea pigs when she accidentally pricked herself with the syringe. Presnyakova was immediately hospitalized under strict isolation so she would not infect her coworkers. She developed Ebola symptoms one week later and died on May 19.

Joseph B. McCormick will never forget his closest call with Ebola. He was taking a blood sample from a presumed Ebola victim when his syringe slipped. "A moment later, I registered the sting of the needle. I saw now that it had broken the skin at the base of my thumbnail," he recalls. "I had a nauseating feeling. . . . I knew, more than most people, that when you get stuck by a potentially contaminated needle in the midst of a deadly epidemic . . . the odds for survival aren't very good."[9]

McCormick was lucky; the patient did not have Ebola. But McCormick's experience shows just how dangerous this disease can be. Even when proper precautions are taken, one tiny slip can destroy barriers and send Ebola streaming into a previously healthy body.

The Disease Takes Hold

When a virus enters a host, an immune response normally occurs. During this process the body notices the virions, realizes they should not be there, and sends special cells to attack and engulf them. In other words, it fights back against the foreign agents. A virus may gain a temporary foothold and make a person sick for a few days, but the body usually prevails in the end.

Ebola disables this process. Although scientists do not fully understand how the virus accomplishes this, it appears that

An Ebola virus is shown infecting a human liver cell.

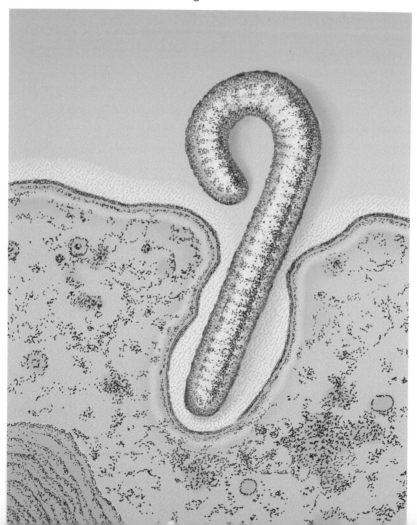

Ebola may mount an attack on the immune system by binding itself to certain white blood cells. The particular cells that are attracted to Ebola happen to be message carriers; their function is to tell the rest of the immune system that something is wrong. Trapped by Ebola virions, however, these cells cannot do their job. The immune system therefore ignores the invaders, leaving them free to multiply.

To copy itself, an Ebola virion uses the spikes on its protein shell to cling to a living cell. It releases its RNA into the cell along with a substance that activates the cell's copying function. The cell quickly produces an identical twin of the Ebola RNA. It copies the copies, then reproduces those copies as well, picking up speed as more and more RNA strands become available. Increasingly jammed with virus, the cell sickens and swells until finally it can hold no more. It bursts open and spews masses of Ebola into the body, dying in the process.

The new virions drift away from the wrecked cell. Because the body's immune system is still oblivious to the invasion, nothing stops them. They eventually come into contact with healthy cells, attach themselves, and inject their RNA, thus starting the multiplication process all over again. More and more virions are produced, more and more cells die, and the Ebola infection worsens with each passing hour.

Changes Inside the Body

Due to details of its shape, the Ebola virus attaches most easily to certain types of cells. The cells that build blood-vessel walls seem to be particularly prone to the virus's ravages, especially in the early stages of an infection. Virions stick to these cells and activate the replication process. The sick cells soon burst and die, releasing new virions that infect neighboring cells. It does not take long for this process to damage a victim's circulatory system. Holes and rips appear as the person's veins, arteries, and capillaries get thinner and weaker, and blood starts oozing into the surrounding tissues.

This blood, of course, is swimming with Ebola. Now loose within the body's connective tissue, the virus starts to wreak new havoc on its victim. In particular, it attacks and destroys

The Ebola Virus Attacks

The body becomes infected with the Ebola virus when it is exposed to infected bodily fluids such as blood, mucus, diarrhea, semen, or vomit.

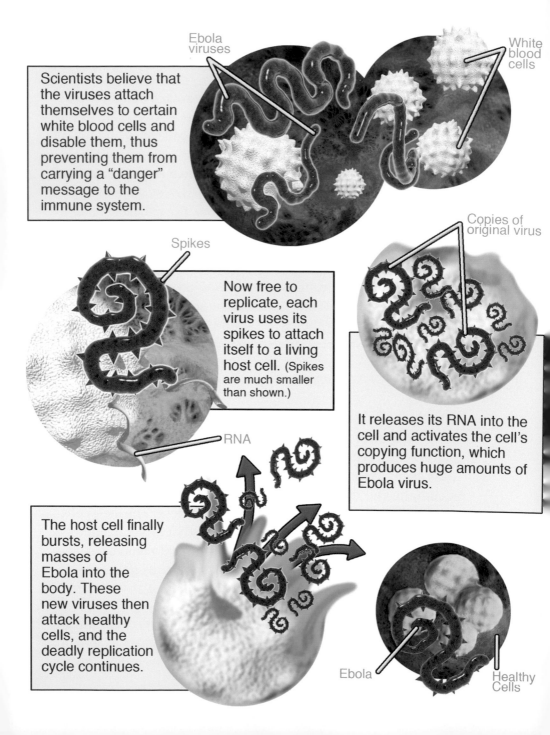

Ebola viruses

White blood cells

Scientists believe that the viruses attach themselves to certain white blood cells and disable them, thus preventing them from carrying a "danger" message to the immune system.

Spikes

Copies of original virus

Now free to replicate, each virus uses its spikes to attach itself to a living host cell. (Spikes are much smaller than shown.)

RNA

It releases its RNA into the cell and activates the cell's copying function, which produces huge amounts of Ebola virus.

The host cell finally bursts, releasing masses of Ebola into the body. These new viruses then attack healthy cells, and the deadly replication cycle continues.

Ebola

Healthy Cells

the fatty substances that flesh out the skin and support everything inside the body. A slow internal collapse begins.

Meanwhile, other Ebola virions stay in the bloodstream and travel to the victim's vital organs. Scientists have not been able to study human organs in the throes of infection, so they do not know exactly what happens next. They do know, however, that the results are devastating. The cells that line the stomach and intestines are destroyed, and they start to flake off. The lungs become spongy and leak blood. The heart and brain are damaged; the kidneys and liver start to die. Upon autopsy, these organs show shocking signs of decay. Richard Preston vividly describes the liver of one disease victim: "[It] had ceased functioning several days before he died. It was yellow, and parts of it had liquefied—it looked like the liver of a three-day-old cadaver. It was as if [the patient] had become a corpse before his death."[10]

As the disease progresses, the situation inside the victim's body becomes increasingly unstable. The blood pressure plummets as fluid seeps freely out of the veins and arteries, and the pulse quickens as the heart tries to compensate. At the same time, the body activates its clotting function in an effort to stop the massive bleeding. Dark chunks of congealed blood build up along the vessel walls and inside the patient's organs. Now clogging the already traumatized system, the clots themselves become part of the problem.

By the time a patient reaches this point, he or she is desperately ill. The body may shut down at any moment from heart failure, septic shock (the simultaneous failure of multiple organs), or stroke. These developments are known informally as "crashing out," and they are always fatal in Ebola patients.

It Starts with a Headache

All of Ebola's internal actions cause external symptoms—eventually. At first, however, there is no outward sign that a person has contracted the disease. It usually takes four to ten days before an Ebola victim develops noticeable symptoms. Occasionally the incubation period is as short as two days or as long as twenty-one, but these extremes are not typical.

The first symptom of Ebola is often a splitting headache, which intensifies until the entire head and neck are pounding with pain.

The incubation period ends abruptly. A seemingly healthy person suddenly develops a fever of around 103 degrees Fahrenheit (39.4°C) as the immune system finally reacts to the infection. He or she complains of a splitting headache, which worsens until the entire head and neck throb with pain. Soon the body's other muscles are in agony, too, as are the joints. The muscles weaken, sometimes to the point of helplessness, and the eyeballs become cherry red as the tiny blood vessels inside them burst.

Gastrointestinal problems develop next. The patient's throat becomes raw and sore, to the point that eating and drinking are impossible. The body is wracked by severe stomach and intestinal pains. The patient feels nauseated, and soon he or she starts to vomit uncontrollably. The vomit is grainy and black with digested blood. Around the same time, the patient begins to suffer from diarrhea. This matter, too, is tarry with blood that has seeped through the intestinal walls. The diarrhea may also carry bits of intestinal lining that have died and sloughed off—something that does not usually happen until a person has been dead for several days.

As the illness progresses, a rash often becomes visible on the body. The rash is caused by blood collecting beneath the victim's skin. If the patient receives an injection at this point, the pooled blood will come pouring out at the injection site. Blood may also start to trickle or even flood from the patient's nose, anus, ears, and eyes as the inside of the body breaks down. This type of hemorrhage does not occur in all Ebola patients. When it does, however, it is a sure sign that death is approaching.

Just before death, an Ebola patient goes into a rapid decline. The mind becomes dull; the patient may slip into a coma. Breathing is rapid and shallow. Because the patient's connective tissues have collapsed, the face appears sunken and expressionless. The body temperature drops into the normal range as the immune system gives up and stops fighting. By this time, explains Preston, "the body [is saturated] with virus particles, from the brain to the skin. . . . An eyedropper of the victim's blood may contain a hundred million particles of virus."[11]

There is no way a human body can withstand this level of attack. Overwhelmed by Ebola, the patient slips into terminal shock and then dies. The entire process has taken just seven to nine days—an incredibly short period for an infectious agent.

There Is No Cure

Ebola is terrifying not just because it works so fast but also because no one knows how to stop it. Although scientists have searched for a cure in laboratories and have tested various treatments on disease victims, nothing so far has been particularly effective.

One early possibility was a drug called ribavirin. Created in the 1970s, ribavirin destroys many viruses, including those that cause influenza, hepatitis, polio, measles, and some hemorrhagic fevers. Virologists once hoped that the drug would be equally effective against Ebola. Unfortunately, this has not proven to be the case. Ebola patients who are injected with ribavirin show no improvement.

Interferon, a natural protein that stops some viruses from multiplying, shows a bit more promise. Combined with other drugs that support the immune system, interferon seems to delay death in Ebola-infected monkeys. In addition, an interferon cocktail may have saved the lives of four Russian scientists who were exposed to Ebola through a laboratory accident. Although there is no proof that the drug had any effect, all four scientists did recover—an encouraging result that merits further study. The practical use of interferon or any other anti-Ebola drug, however, is still a distant dream.

Because no known medicine can cure Ebola, scientists are experimenting with ways to help patients cure themselves. One way of doing this is to introduce plasma (the liquid part of blood) from recovered Ebola victims into current patients. Scientists reason that the plasma has already "learned" how to fight Ebola through a previous exposure and can therefore boost the patient's flagging immune system. This approach makes sense in theory, but in practice it is not so clear-cut.

A 1995 photo in a Zairean hospital shows an Ebola victim. Poor hospitals cannot afford to provide promising experimental therapies for Ebola.

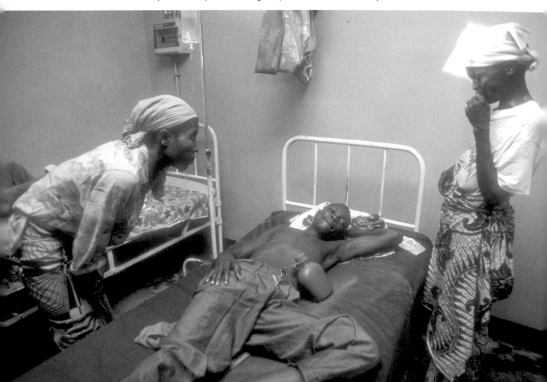

Ebola progresses so quickly that the plasma's antibodies have little time to do their job. Still, there is some evidence that plasma treatment can be helpful. It will undoubtedly be used and studied further during future epidemics.

Plasma treatment and other experimental therapies, however, have one major drawback. Even if they prove to be effective, they probably will never be available at the poor African hospitals where most Ebola victims are treated. In these environments, the best any patient can hope for is careful nursing. By aggressively treating Ebola's symptoms and making the sufferer comfortable, medical professionals can sometimes slow the disease's progress. This delay may give a person's immune system enough time to conquer the illness on its own.

Survivors Suffer

If a patient survives Ebola longer than nine or ten days, chances are good that he or she will recover. The road back to health, however, is far from pleasant. Long, difficult, and often painful, the recovery process takes an enormous toll on those who must endure it.

Restoring the body's balance is the critical first step in Ebola recovery. Most patients have lost a great deal of weight during their illness, and their bodies are severely dehydrated. It takes weeks or even months of careful eating and drinking to reverse the worst of this damage. The process is especially difficult in the early stages of convalescence, when the body is still fighting off the Ebola virus. Most recovering patients shed viral particles for up to five weeks after their illness has run its course. In men, the virus lingers in the semen for two to three months.

Early Ebola convalescence is also marked by severe shedding. Patients look like extreme sunburn victims as their entire skin surface flakes and peels away. Because Ebola damages the cells that hold hairs in place, patients often develop bald patches as well. These events are outward signs of the enormous cleanup task going on inside the body. By casting off dead and dying cells, the body is working to restore itself to health.

Good health, however, may never return to some people. A full year after one major epidemic, a medical journal reported that nearly one-quarter of the 257 survivors were still receiving treatment for various symptoms. Their complaints included abdominal pains, vision and hearing loss, bleeding, mental problems, and overall weakness. Not only did these conditions affect the patients' well-being, they affected their daily lives as well. "Most of the survivors have become poorer because they can no longer work as much as before they became ill. Some are unable to perform simple exercises such as riding a bicycle,"[12] the article reports. For these people, life after Ebola is a daily struggle that may never get easier.

It Could Be Worse

Because of its horror-movie symptoms, its high mortality rate, and its agonizing aftermath, Ebola earns its reputation as the world's most terrifying disease. But many virologists point out that the situation could be much worse. If Ebola spread through the air, epidemics might turn entire continents into burial grounds. It is fortunate for humanity that this is not the case. By isolating known patients, crisis-management teams can easily cut off the main source of an outbreak.

Even a quarantined Ebola patient, of course, has continued contact with medical professionals and sometimes family members as well. If the virus leaped easily from one person to another, it would have plenty of chances to spread. But Ebola does not spread easily. When even the most basic precautions are taken, healthy people who nurse Ebola patients have only a 5 to 10 percent chance of contracting the disease. And there seems to be almost no risk to casual contacts, especially during the incubation period. Ebola carriers sometimes interact with dozens of people before they realize they are sick. As long as no intimate contact occurs, it is rare for these people to become ill.

Ironically, Ebola's exceptional severity is another trait that keeps the virus under control. People with full-blown Ebola are usually too weak to walk, let alone to socialize. Because they cannot get around, their opportunities to transmit the disease are limited. Also, the disease simply kills its victims too quickly. It progresses so rapidly that patients do not have time to infect many others. A virus like HIV, in contrast, can live se-

Conspiracy Theory

Some scientists believe that filoviruses developed in labs, not in nature. Scientist and independent investigator Leonard G. Horowitz is one prominent supporter of this view. According to Horowitz, the process began in the early 1960s, when many scientific agencies were using monkeys as test subjects in disease and vaccine research. Horowitz notes that one major research firm did a great deal of work in Uganda in 1965. Specifically, the firm was studying the viral group known as rhabdoviruses, and as Horowitz points out, "rhabdoviruses . . . were considered by many experts as the germ from which Marburg and Ebola viruses most likely evolved. [In the Uganda studies,] these viruses . . . had been manipulated, mutated, or mixed with other deadly viruses."

The mutated rhabdoviruses were injected into monkeys, many of which died as a result. Most of the survivors were transferred to other facilities, including the one where Marburg first appeared in 1967. The timing, says Horowitz, was suspiciously perfect. He believes that these monkeys had contracted Marburg as a direct result of the 1965 experiments. Researchers were not aware they had created a killer disease until the virus leaped to a human victim.

Leonard G. Horowitz, *Emerging Viruses: AIDS & Ebola—Nature, Accident, or Intentional?* Sandpoint, ID: Tetrahedron, 1999, pp. 445, 471.

cretly in a carrier for decades before symptoms appear. The carrier may infect countless people during this long incubation period.

Ebola's Hiding Place

HIV is one example of a virus that is well adapted to living inside humans. Ebola, on the other hand, is not. By killing within weeks, Ebola destroys its human victims before it even has time to settle in. This is a bad survival strategy for a virus. As scientist Frank Ryan puts it, "If the virus wins this war . . . all

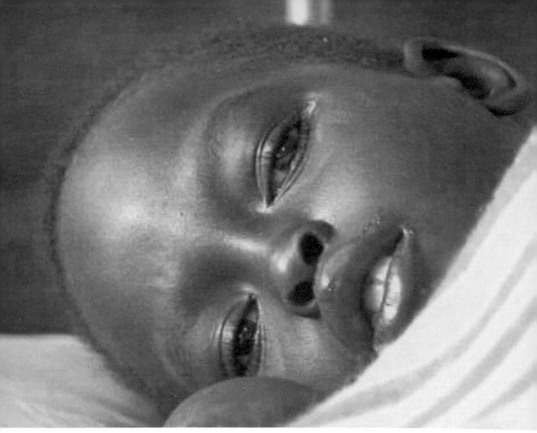

Since Ebola victims like this youngster are too weak to socialize, opportunities for them to transmit the disease are limited.

of its victims die. . . . Over time this also condemns the virus to extinction."[13] In other words, it is not in a virus's best interest to kill its host too quickly.

For this reason, many types of viruses have learned to coexist with specific animal hosts. The virus that causes bubonic plague, for example, is found inside certain fleas, and the virus that causes rabies can be carried by bats. Coexisting viruses are harmless to their carriers. If they infect other creatures, however, the results may be devastating. In Ryan's words, "What we actually observe is a striking difference between the aggressive behavior of a virus in a totally novel host . . . when compared to its seemingly benign behavior in its long-established host."[14]

There is every reason to believe that Ebola follows this pattern. But despite decades of searching, no one has been able to pinpoint Ebola's natural reservoir. Until Ebola's host is discovered, the virus will remain in hiding, and the human population will wait helplessly for it to reappear.

Ebola Reappears

After the Zaire and Sudan epidemics of 1976, scientists did their best to find Ebola's natural hiding place. They focused their efforts on the insect and animal samples that had been taken from the cotton factory in Nzara. Hundreds of blood and tissue specimens were analyzed as virologists hunted for any sign of the virus.

When scientists began their investigation, they were certain they would find Ebola lurking somewhere in the cotton factory samples. They started to lose hope, however, as the months wore on without success. Finally they had to admit that they had failed in their task. For now, Ebola had disappeared, but this did not mean it was gone for good. Health officials waited anxiously for the disease to make its next appearance.

They did not have to wait long. In June 1977 Ebola struck again in Zaire, claiming just one victim before vanishing again. This incident, although isolated, was alarming to the world medical community. It proved that Ebola was still hiding in the depths of the Congo and that it was still finding its way into human victims.

Sudan, 1979

The disease next showed itself in 1979. On August 2 a forty-five-year-old man was admitted to the Nzara hospital in Sudan—the same hospital that had treated many victims of the 1976 epidemic. The patient's complaints included a high fever, vomiting, and diarrhea. The sick man soon developed internal

The body of an Ebola victim lies outside a morgue in Zaire, where the virus briefly reappeared in 1977.

bleeding as well. Despite the best efforts of the hospital staff, the patient died on August 5.

Even though Nzara's medical staff had dealt with Ebola before, they did not recognize the man's symptoms, and they did not take any special precautions while treating their patient. They were not especially worried about the case. But that changed in late August, when several more patients with hemorrhagic symptoms arrived at the hospital. One of these patients had been in the hospital just a few weeks earlier with a stomach problem, and he had shared a room with the now-dead man. Another patient had visited her husband in the hospital while the index patient was on the ward. The staff began to suspect that Ebola was at work. Their suspicions were all but confirmed when they learned that three relatives of the first patient had developed bleeding fevers and died at home. Frightened that a new epidemic was brewing, the staff notified international authorities of the situation.

The district was quarantined in early September, but this action did not stop the outbreak from spreading. Two nurses in the Nzara hospital developed Ebola and died. Family members of previous patients became sick as well. Worried that the outbreak might spread even farther, a team sponsored by the World Health Organization (WHO) arrived to take control of the situation on September 22. The team eventually managed to contain the outbreak, but not before thirty-four people had contracted Ebola. Twenty-two of these people died of the disease—a mortality rate of 65 percent.

By shutting down the epidemic, the WHO team had accomplished its primary goal. Now the scientists turned to another task: determining the virus's origin. They were surprised to learn that the index case in the current epidemic had worked at the Nzara cotton factory, just like the index case in the 1976 epidemic. The scientists went to the factory and spoke to its manager, and they examined the factory's attendance records to see how often employees had been sick. But these efforts did not yield any clues. In a follow-up report, the scientists admitted they had "failed to incriminate the factory as an active source of infection."[15] The investigation had reached a dead end, and Ebola had gone into hiding once again.

Ebola Comes to America

After the 1979 outbreak, Ebola was not seen for ten years, and virologists started to relax. But they were about to get a shock. In 1989 Ebola reappeared—not in Zaire, not in Sudan, but in a bustling suburb of Washington, D.C.

The incident began in early October, when a shipment of one hundred monkeys from the Philippines arrived in the United States. The monkeys were meant to be used in scientific experiments. Before they could be distributed to laboratories, though, they were required by law to be quarantined for thirty days. They were sent to a holding facility in Reston, Virginia, where they were placed in special containment rooms.

The monkeys looked fine at first. Soon, however, they started to get sick. By November 1 many of the monkeys had died. Dan Dalgard, the veterinarian on duty, thought the monkeys were dying of simian hemorrhagic fever (SHF)—a disease with symptoms similar to Ebola and other human hemorrhagic

Supposedly healthy Philippine monkeys like these were brought to the United States in 1989 for use in experiments. Scientists soon learned that they were infected with Ebola.

fevers. This disease is deadly to monkeys but harmless to humans. Still, Dalgard decided to keep the monkeys in quarantine until he knew for sure what was making them sick.

By November 13 more monkeys had died, many others had fallen ill, and Dalgard still did not know why. He was particularly concerned about the fact that the disease was spreading from room to room, which suggested that it was traveling through the air. Confused and alarmed, the vet placed a call to the nearby U.S. Army Medical Research Institute of Infectious Diseases (USAMRIID). He arranged to send blood and tissue samples from the sick animals for analysis in USAMRIID's laboratories. Upon examination, the samples did indeed show signs of SHF, but they carried something else as well. The samples were teeming with Ebola virus.

The two virologists who noticed the virus immediately took their findings to C.J. Peters, the chief of USAMRIID's Disease Assessment Division. They showed Peters the pictures they had taken through the electron microscope. Peters still remembers this moment vividly: "'What does this look like to you?' [they asked me]. I saw rod-like particles in the cells, some curved at the end like a shepherd's crook, others in bizarrely twisted shapes. 'It looks like a filovirus,' I responded apprehensively."[16]

The scientists were frightened. Ebola was the deadliest virus ever discovered, and here it was in one of the world's busiest cities. All three men knew that an epidemic of massive proportions might be brewing. Peters says today, "There was no need for any of the three of us to say anything out loud, but we were

---

A Monkey Plague

Ebola does not just affect human beings. The virus is equally deadly to monkeys. Since the mid-1990s Ebola has killed an estimated one-third of the world's gorillas along with tens of thousands of chimps. In the hardest-hit areas, 90 percent of the local monkey populations have been wiped out.

Until recently scientists believed that Ebola was found throughout certain monkeys' territories. Epidemics popped up randomly when the monkeys caught the disease from an unknown carrier. According to a virologist named Peter Walsh, however, Ebola epidemics are not random at all. Walsh believes that the disease has been rippling outward from a single starting point, wavelike, since its emergence. When the wave reaches a new area, it immediately starts to burn through the monkey population.

Walsh's theory, if it is correct, could be good news. If Ebola's progress can be predicted, scientists might be able to protect monkey populations before the disease arrives. In particular, a large group of apes in Congo's Odzala National Park—which will feel the first effects of the theoretical wave in three to four years—might be saved. So far, however, Walsh has not been able to raise money for a prevention effort. "In three or four years it will be too late. The apes will be gone," he said in November 2005.

Quoted in Debora Mackenzie, "Great Apes Face Ebola Oblivion," *New Scientist*, November 5, 2005, p. 8.

all thinking the same thing. 'Could this finally be the big one we've been dreading our entire careers?'"[17]

A Lucky Escape

Peters immediately contacted the Centers for Disease Control and Prevention in Atlanta. Officials from USAMRIID and the CDC met and decided to split responsibility for the situation. The CDC would take care of any human victims, and USAMRIID would deal with the monkeys.

Dealing with the monkeys meant euthanizing them—even the healthy ones. The danger was too severe to allow even one monkey to live. So on December 1, USAMRIID sent a containment team to the monkey house in Reston. The team donned protective suits and helmets and entered the facility. They sedated the monkeys and took blood samples, then injected the euthanasia drug. Soon the monkeys were dead.

Like the Ebola-infected Philippine monkeys being put to death in this 1997 photo, the monkeys carrying the Ebola-Reston virus were euthanized in 1989.

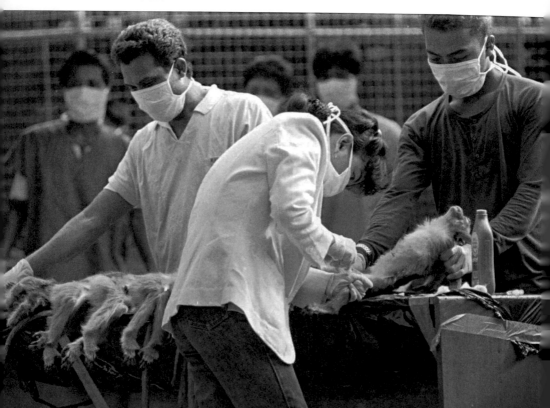

Ebola in the Media

In 1994 Ebola received a huge amount of publicity when a book called *The Hot Zone* was published. Written by Richard Preston, the book explains the origins and symptoms of Marburg and Ebola hemorrhagic fevers. It also describes in detail Ebola's 1989 outbreak in Reston, Virginia. Subtitled *A Terrifying True Story*, Preston's book captured the public's imagination and spent thirty weeks on bestseller lists in the United States. Experts have mixed feelings about *The Hot Zone*, which some say is overly dramatic. Overall, however, the book is usually considered to be a colorful but solid work of nonfiction.

The same cannot be said of the 1995 movie *Outbreak*, which tells the story of a fictional Ebola-like virus that strikes a California town. To stop the deadly disease from spreading, the U.S. Army prepares to bomb the town and everyone in it. Before this can happen, however, the lead character whips up a cure, then leaps into an airplane and blocks the army bomber from doing its job.

Although *Outbreak* was implausible, it was successful at the box office. The film's subject matter interested the public partly because of the Ebola epidemic in Kikwit, which erupted during the movie's theater run.

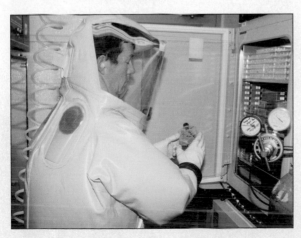

A researcher in protective gear works with the Ebola-Reston virus, which received widespread media attention after publication of *The Hot Zone*.

The operation was grisly and depressing, but when it was all over, officials were convinced it had been worthwhile. Disaster had been averted without a single human victim—or so it seemed.

Virologists later learned through blood analysis, however, that four animal handlers who worked at the facility had been infected after all. None of the handlers had developed Ebola symptoms. It appeared that the Reston virus, although deadly to monkeys, was a new type of Ebola that did not make people sick. The new strain was dubbed Ebola-Reston after its place of discovery.

After the Reston incident ended, health officials traced the sick monkeys to a trader in the Philippines. They searched and searched for an African connection—they thought, for instance, that the monkeys might have come into contact with African animals during shipment—but no link could be found. Virologists finally concluded that the new Ebola strain was not African at all. It was native to Asia, a whole new continent for the virus.

The virus's Asian origin proved just as mysterious as its African cousin's reservoir. Although scientists knew where the infected monkeys had lived, they could not figure out how the animals had contracted Ebola. This failure was very frustrating to top officials, who could only watch helplessly as Ebola's trail grew cold yet again. C.J. Peters describes the general feeling in the medical community: "The Reston episode had an unsatisfactory, unfinished feeling to it; we never found out where the virus came from. We were gratified by our ability to analyze what was happening and contain it, but none of us felt we'd achieved anything that was going to give us a jump on the problem in the future."[18] Ebola was gone, and there was no telling when it might reappear.

More Dead Monkeys

After the Reston outbreak, no confirmed cases of Ebola were reported for another five years. In 1994, however, an Ebola-like disease started to sicken chimpanzees in the Tai Forest, a rain forest region in southwest Côte d'Ivoire (Ivory Coast),

Africa. One chimpanzee troop had lost twenty of its eighty members by November of that year.

Scientists wanted to know what was killing the chimps. They recovered the bodies of two dead animals and took them to a laboratory for study and analysis. Three scientists also did a field autopsy on a chimpanzee corpse that was found on November 16, 1994. Tissue samples from this monkey were sent to the Pasteur Institute in Paris, where they tested positive for a never-before-seen type of Ebola. This new type of Ebola, the fourth to be discovered, was named Ebola-Côte d'Ivoire.

Unlike Ebola-Reston, Ebola-Côte d'Ivoire is able to infect human beings. This fact became clear on November 24, when one of the scientists involved in the November 16 autopsy developed a high fever, diarrhea, and a rash. The scientist had worn latex gloves during the procedure, but the gloves were not in good condition. It is believed that infected chimpanzee blood either got through the gloves or spattered into the scientist's

A young chimpanzee is pictured in the Tai Forest, Côte d'Ivoire. In 1994, chimps in the region were found to carry a new type of Ebola virus.

eyes. One way or the other, the virus entered the scientist's body and began to multiply.

The scientist was immediately transported to her native Switzerland for treatment. Swiss doctors administered fluids and minerals to relieve the patient's dehydration, but other than that, there was little they could do from a medical perspective. Thanks partly to around-the-clock nursing care, however, the scientist conquered the virus on her own after a two-week battle. The disease's effects lingered for a long time, but the scientist eventually recovered from her brush with Ebola.

Some Ebola victims in the western African nation of Gabon were not so lucky. In December 1994 the Zaire strain of the Ebola virus surfaced in a gold-mining camp there. The first wave of the epidemic consisted of gold miners and their close contacts. The second wave occurred after the gold miners vis-

In the Democratic Republic of the Congo, outside Kikwit Hospital, boys with their faces covered as protection against Ebola wait for the body of a relative dead of the virus.

ited and contaminated a local hospital. By the time the outbreak ended, fifty-two people had contracted Ebola. Of these, thirty-one had lost their lives.

Kikwit, 1995

As the Côte d'Ivoire and Gabon incidents died down, a new situation began to brew nearby. Unknown to authorities, Ebola was loose again in Zaire, which was now called the Democratic Republic of the Congo (DRC).

The epidemic probably began in early January 1995. At this time a man known in medical literature as C1 appeared at the hospital in Kikwit, a large town of about two hundred thousand people, with fever and other Ebola symptoms. The hospital staff did not suspect Ebola, and they did not take any special precautions. The patient died on January 13, but not before causing an outbreak—which also went unrecognized—in the hospital's maternity ward.

The first important case of the epidemic came to light on April 10. On that day a lab technician named Kimfumu was scheduled to undergo intestinal surgery. Kimfumu had a fever, and doctors thought he had an internal injury. But the doctors did not discover any injury during surgery. Instead, they found that the patient's intestines and other organs were swimming with blood. They did what they could and closed up the patient, who became steadily sicker until he died on April 14.

After Kimfumu's death, the situation worsened very quickly. Most of the medical staff who had cared for Kimfumu in the operating theater or afterward came down with fevers, headaches, and other Ebola symptoms. The friends and families of these people started to get sick, too. The circle of infection widened, and the death toll began to mount.

By the end of April, top local authorities had been alerted to the situation. They soon determined that a viral hemorrhagic fever was responsible for the outbreak. They immediately shut down Kikwit's main hospital along with the rest of the town's health centers and laboratories, hoping to stop the virus from spreading. They also collected blood samples and sent them to the CDC. When the samples tested positive for Ebola, the

DRC's government officially declared the epidemic and asked WHO to coordinate an international response.

A WHO team arrived in Kikwit on May 11 and discovered a chaotic situation. Pierre Rollin, a CDC official and a member of the team, remembers the scene clearly: "When we arrived [at Kikwit Hospital], it was very bad. People were vomiting; there was diarrhea and blood all over the floors and walls. The dead were lying among the living."[19] Family members were walking freely in and out of the festering wards, possibly carrying the virus as they went.

The situation was bad in other areas as well. Ebola had already spread to several nearby towns, where it was affecting hundreds of people. Thanks in large part to quarantines and other official actions, however, the epidemic died down quickly. The last-known patient died on July 16, and the outbreak was declared over forty-two days later (twice the longest-known incubation period for the disease). Officially, 315 people had contracted Ebola, and 250 had died. The virus had claimed the lives of 80 percent of those it infected.

Lessons Learned from Kikwit

The Kikwit outbreak was the biggest Ebola epidemic to hit since the disease had first appeared in 1976. As in the earlier outbreaks, the virus spread fast and killed quickly. But even though Ebola was just as deadly as ever, it did not terrify scientists quite as much this time around. Medical professionals now knew enough about Ebola to feel fairly sure they could control the situation. Managing the Kikwit epidemic was dirty, discouraging work, to be sure, but it was also an exciting opportunity to learn more about the mysterious Ebola virus.

Some of the scientists' findings were purely medical. For the first time, doctors were able to observe a large number of Ebola patients in a hospital setting. The doctors recorded each patient's personal information, including age and sex. They determined how each patient had contracted Ebola. They also charted the course of each patient's illness as the days went by, carefully noting each symptom along with its timing. By doing these things, the doctors were able to create a complete pic-

At Kikwit Hospital (pictured in 1995), where scientists worked with large numbers of Ebola patients in a hospital setting, critical information about the virus was discovered.

ture of the disease and its course—something that had been impossible up to that point. Today, the Kikwit findings are considered the authoritative Ebola reference for doctors everywhere.

Medical knowledge was not the only important thing to come out of the Kikwit epidemic. Doctors and investigators also learned many practical things about dealing with an Ebola outbreak. In a 1999 WHO paper, the organization laid out some of these findings. WHO called in particular for stronger infectious disease surveillance and control around the world:

> Weakened . . . surveillance in the Kikwit area of the DRC permitted the 1995 outbreak of Ebola virus to continue through many generations and over a period of at least 12 weeks before it came to the attention of local health authorities. . . . Training and development of skills in surveillance, prevention, and disease control are essential.[20]

WHO also recommended creating international supply stockpiles for emergency use, providing more information to government officials during an outbreak, and involving more international partners in future Ebola response efforts.

In the same paper, WHO noted the increasing presence of the media in emergency medical situations. The organization contended that journalists and photographers made the investigators' work more difficult in many ways:

> [They] arrived in a group on a small chartered plane and within minutes, had forcefully violated many of the protective barriers in order to get that "most sensational story or photograph." Ethical standards, such as patient consent to be filmed, were breached; cultural sensitivity was ignored as crews filmed family members caring for the sick or burying the dead; inaccurate reports were dispatched; and the work of those caring for patients and containing the epidemic was disrupted. . . . Prices for renting vehicles necessary for epidemic control from the already limited fleet more than doubled once the press arrived, and accommodations for newly arriving members of the international commission became scarce and difficult to find.[21]

Despite these problems, the media's presence had many positive effects. In particular, worldwide publicity raised awareness of the outbreak and made it easier for the investigators to obtain some of the resources they needed. So the goal for field staff, stated the WHO report, should be "to capitalize on the powerful positive role that the global media could play and to accommodate their needs without detracting from the primary mission of patient care, epidemic control, and research."[22] By doing these things, investigators could ensure that matters proceeded more smoothly during future Ebola outbreaks.

Ebola Since 1996

Future outbreaks, unfortunately, arrived much sooner than anyone anticipated. During 1996 alone, two Ebola outbreaks occurred in Gabon. The first episode ran from February to April and claimed twenty-one victims. The second outbreak began in July and continued all the way into 1997, eventually taking the lives of forty-five people.

Since the year 2000, six other small Ebola outbreaks have occurred. In Gabon, the virus erupted again in 2001 and claimed fifty-three lives. In 2001, 2003, and 2005, epidemics struck in Congo, a small nation to the west of the DRC, killing a total of eighty-two people. And Sudan lost a total of twelve people during two outbreaks in 2004 and 2005.

Ebola Outbreak Chronology

Year	Country	Virus	Cases	Deaths	Fatality
1976	Sudan	Ebola-Sudan	284	151	53%
1976	Zaire (DRC)	Ebola-Zaire	318	280	88%
1979	Sudan	Ebola-Sudan	34	22	65%
1994	Gabon	Ebola-Zaire	52	31	60%
1994	Côte d'Ivoire	Ebola-Côte d'Ivoire	1	0	0%
1995	Democratic Republic of Congo	Ebola-Zaire	315	250	80%
1996	Gabon	Ebola-Zaire	37	21	57%
1996–1997	Gabon	Ebola-Zaire	60	45	74%
2000–2001	Uganda	Ebola-Sudan	425	224	53%
2001–2002	Gabon	Ebola-Zaire	65	53	82%
2001–2002	Republic of Congo	Ebola-Zaire	59	44	75%
2002–2003	Republic of Congo	Ebola-Zaire	143	128	89%
2003	Republic of Congo	Ebola-Zaire	35	29	83%
2004	Sudan	Ebola-Sudan	17	7	41%
2005	Sudan	Unknown	19	5	26%
2005	Republic of Congo	Unknown	12	9	75%

Data Source: World Health Organization.

In addition to these minor episodes, two major epidemics have occurred since the turn of the century. The first of these outbreaks took place in Uganda, which borders both Sudan and the DRC. Between October 2000 and January 2001, officials recorded 425 cases of Ebola and 224 deaths in this small country. The second large epidemic shook Congo from December 2002 to April 2003. During the course of the outbreak, 143 people became ill and 128 died—a shocking 89 percent mortality rate.

It is clear from these statistics that Ebola today is just as deadly as ever. It is also evident that over the past few years the virus has begun erupting more and more frequently in the areas it affects. This is bad news for residents of Ebola-prone regions, who will probably suffer through more outbreaks in the near future. At present, the world medical community can do nothing to prevent these outbreaks from happening. Officials can only wait, watch, and be ready to act the next time Ebola makes an appearance.

CHAPTER FOUR

Containing Ebola

When Ebola first erupted in 1976, it was completely unknown to scientists. The anonymous virus was able to wreak havoc in large part because it caught health officials by surprise. Early on, when the virus might have been stopped easily, no one in authority knew about the situation. Later, when officials realized they had a major problem on their hands, no one knew quite what to do about it. Between the slow world reaction and the clumsy response, the epidemic became severe before it finally died out.

Today the world medical community knows much more about dealing with Ebola than it did in 1976. International medical organizations have created step-by-step guidelines for handling an epidemic, from discovery to aftermath and beyond. Containment teams follow these guidelines closely when they arrive at the site of an Ebola outbreak. By doing so, they bring order to a potentially explosive situation.

Identifying the Disease

The first step in controlling an Ebola outbreak is identifying early cases of the disease. However, it is not always easy to do this. In its initial stages, Ebola hemorrhagic fever resembles many other illnesses. One report points out:

> Recognition of [Ebola] in endemic zones presents a major challenge since the early signs and symptoms are non-specific and similar to those of more common tropical

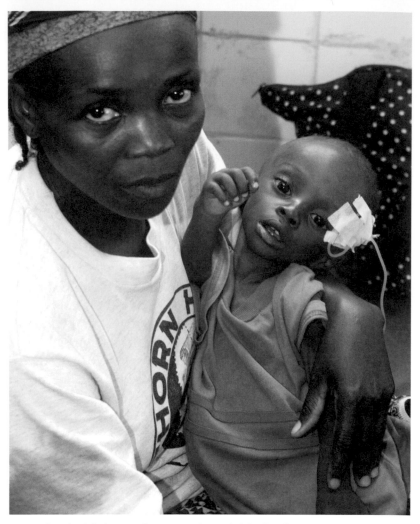

A mother holds her malaria-stricken child. The first symptoms of Ebola infection resemble those of malaria and other illnesses, making early diagnosis difficult.

infections, including typhoid fever and malaria. Furthermore . . . even after a fatal case with haemorrhage, the diagnosis may not be considered until several patients are observed simultaneously.[23]

For these reasons, Ebola cases often go unidentified in the first days of an epidemic.

Another challenge in spotting Ebola involves poorly trained hospital personnel. The doctors and nurses at many African medical centers have only the most basic medical education, and some of them have no formal training at all. While these people have a wealth of personal experience to draw upon, they usually do not have the knowledge or resources of their counterparts in more developed parts of the world. Ebola is likely to go unrecognized if it strikes in this medical environment.

To improve this situation, international organizations are working to educate medical professionals in equatorial Africa about the disease. They are doing this mostly through printed literature. The Special Pathogens Branch of the Centers for Disease Control, for instance, has created a pamphlet that describes Ebola's symptoms and lays out ways to identify the virus. In particular, the CDC advises health professionals in Ebola-prone areas to pay special attention to patients with mysterious fevers. If the source of a fever cannot be identified within three days, the patient should be isolated and monitored carefully. A fever patient who starts to bleed or goes into shock, says the pamphlet, should be assumed to have Ebola or another viral hemorrhagic fever.

If local health professionals do not report Ebola, computers may be able to do the job. As the World Health Organization (WHO) notes, "With the advent of modern communication technologies, many initial outbreak reports now originate in the electronic media and electronic discussion groups."[24] To form these resources, Health Canada, together with WHO, has developed a tool called the Global Public Health Intelligence Network. This tool continuously searches Internet-based news wires and Web sites for information about Ebola and other threats to public health. It summarizes anything it discovers for human officials, who then scan the findings for signs of trouble.

Worldwide Response

When any medical professional suspects Ebola, he or she is responsible for contacting local officials. These officials pass the information to the nation's governing body and to the World Health Organization as well. WHO in turn alerts key agencies, such as the CDC, the Centre for Applied Microbiology and Research at Porton Down, U.S. Army Medical Research Institute of Infectious Diseases, the International Red

Level 4

Laboratories that handle biological materials are ranked accord-ing to their safety level. Level 1 labs routinely handle substances that do not cause disease in humans. Level 2 and 3 labs are safe for the study of progressively more dangerous materials. The highest biosafety level of all, Level 4, or BSL-4, is reserved for Ebola and other deadly pathogens that cannot be cured. Scien-tists who work in BSL-4 labs go to extraordinary lengths to avoid direct contact with these materials.

C.J. Peters, a well-known virologist who has headed divisions at both USAMRIID and the CDC, describes the Level 4 experience in his book, Virus Hunter.

Before you can even be authorized, you have to be intensively trained and you have to receive inoculations against anything potentially inside that we have inoculations for. Next, you go into a locker room and take off all your clothing, even your un-derwear. Then you put on a clean scrub suit and surgical gloves, followed by the full-body "space suit.". . . Then you [and your lab partner] check for rips, tears, or anything that doesn't seem quite right. Only then are you ready to go through the last air lock into Level 4. . . .

Once inside Level 4, you hook up your air hose to one of the overhead supplies and you immediately hear the din of rushing air

Cross, and any relevant local organizations. It also directly contacts the local doctors who are handling the presumed out-break. The doctors receive instructions for safely obtaining, packing, and shipping blood and tissue samples to laborato-ries where they can be analyzed.

Once the samples reach the CDC or another lab, they are tested to see if they contain Ebola virus. If the samples test positive, WHO mobilizes a containment team. This team is drawn from the Global Outbreak Alert and Response Network (GOARN), a group of 110 institutions that share their exper-

all around you. Communication with your lab partner and speaking on the telephone are difficult, sometimes impossible. If you must speak, you may have to momentarily turn off your air supply, which is not a comfortable feeling. The environment within the hot suit is so claustrophobic and the noise within the helmet so loud and intrusive that some people can never get used to it.

C.J. Peters and Mark Olshaker, *Virus Hunter: Thirty Years of Battling Hot Viruses Around the World*. New York: Anchor, 1997, pp. 252–53.

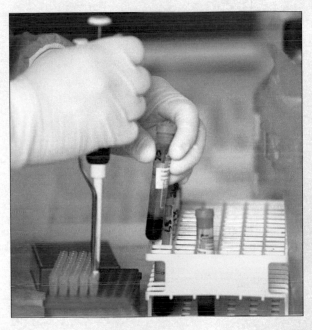

In a Level 4 lab, where lethal pathogens are studied, a CDC researcher checks blood samples for the presence of Ebola.

tise during outbreaks or epidemics. GOARN was created in 2000 to improve WHO's response to Ebola and other deadly diseases. At that time, explains WHO, officials realized that "no single institution or country has all of the capacities to respond to international public health emergencies caused by epidemics and by new and emerging infectious diseases."[25] By pooling GOARN's resources, WHO can pull together the right mix of experts for any outbreak situation.

The chosen experts act quickly. They start to pack their bags, assemble any equipment they think they will need, and make travel arrangements as soon as they receive WHO's call. Within hours they are on their way. It usually takes twenty-four hours or less for the complete team to gather at the outbreak site.

The First Step: Education

After the team members arrive, they head for the local hospital. When they get there, they almost always discover that the hospital has become the area's main source of Ebola. Transmission of Ebola or any other illness in a hospital setting is called nosocomial transmission. It occurs when one patient infects the medical staff, other patients, or both, and it is extremely common when basic sanitary precautions are not taken. A doctor or a nurse has contact with an Ebola patient, picks up a virus load, and carries it to another patient. Soon the entire hospital is teeming with Ebola.

Nosocomial transmission has played a part in nearly every Ebola outbreak. It is a continuing problem in Africa, where small hospitals are often run under near-primitive conditions. Because money is always tight, hospitals cannot always afford latex gloves and other protective equipment that would keep doctors and nurses safe. Even soap and running water may be in short supply. In addition, patients are often crowded together in dirty communal wards. With poor hygiene and cramped conditions, these hospitals easily explode into Ebola breeding grounds.

During the Sudan epidemic of 1976, the Nzara hospital served as one such breeding ground. In her book *The Coming Plague*, writer Laurie Garrett comments on the situation:

> What might have otherwise been individual illness, limited to one or two cases of Ebola, was magnified in a hospital setting in which unsterile equipment and needles were used repeatedly on numerous patients. Nzara Hospital couldn't [even] afford mattresses. . . . It could hardly be expected to throw away every single plastic syringe simply because it had previously been used.[26]

Under usual circumstances this behavior is understandable, if not ideal. During an Ebola outbreak, however, it cannot be

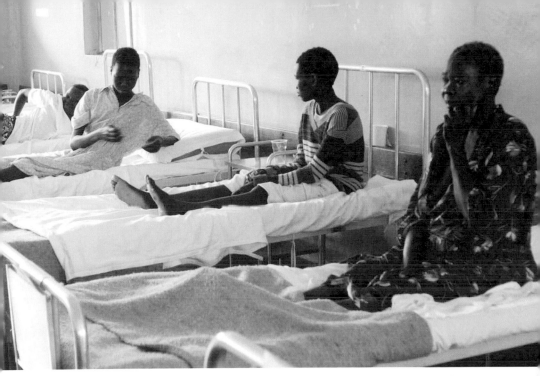

Ebola patients housed in primitive hospital wards can infect each other, as well as the medical staff.

allowed to continue. So the containment team's first job is to speak with hospital staff and make sure they know how to handle Ebola without spreading it to other patients or catching it themselves. Team members give the staff protective clothing such as gowns, gloves, masks, and rubber boots, along with instructions for when and how to use these items. They teach staff members how to disinfect spills, waste, reusable equipment, and laundry, and they discuss the safe disposal of contaminated materials. By taking these simple steps, the medical staff can stop new cases of Ebola from developing within the hospital's walls.

The Next Step: Isolation

After the containment team has spoken with the hospital staff, it must isolate any suspected Ebola patients. Private rooms are not available in many African hospitals, so the team usually arranges one group ward. During a large outbreak, many beds are pushed close together to make room for all the sick people. Sheets or shower curtains are hung between the beds to keep patients' bodily fluids from splashing onto one another.

The air conditioning, if there is any, is turned off to avoid the smallest chance of spreading Ebola by way of the hospital's air handling system.

Once the isolation ward has been created, it is shut off from the outside world. The containment team places warning signs all around the ward. It may block doors and windows with rope or tape to reinforce the message. If an outbreak is especially severe, the team may even hire security guards to prevent unauthorized people from entering the ward. As the CDC points out in one publication, "This is critical for maintaining strict isolation and protecting the community."[27]

From a Western perspective, posting armed guards in a hospital seems extreme. But it is sometimes necessary in Africa, where families expect full access to sick relatives. In the words of Joseph B. McCormick, "When a patient is admitted to a hospital, his family practically moves in with him."[28] People are

In 1995, to protect the outside community from infection by Ebola, armed guards controlled the entrance to Kikwit hospital.

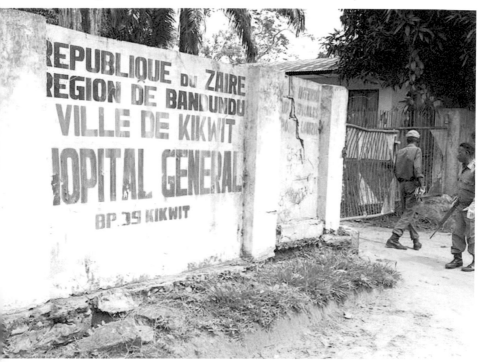

shocked and angry when medical officials tell them they cannot enter the isolation ward. They may ignore the doctors' advice and visit their family members anyway. When this situation arises, hiring security guards is a logical and essential choice.

Despite the risk of infection, one or two family members are sometimes allowed to visit Ebola patients. The chosen caregivers receive gowns, masks, and gloves, and they are educated about the proper way to handle an Ebola victim. By allowing these people to enter the ward, the containment team makes the quarantine easier for other family members to accept. Doctors do not like this compromise, but they realize it is necessary. "If I had a choice, I would prohibit it . . . but that's not possible here,"[29] sighed one doctor during the Kikwit epidemic of 1995.

Stopping the Spread

After the local hospitals are safe, containment officials turn their attention to the community at large. They ask around for news of Ebola victims who have not sought treatment. It is critical to find and isolate these people so they cannot make other people sick. Dealing with Ebola outside the hospital, however, can be the hardest part of a containment job. It is not always easy to find Ebola patients in the community. Also, even when these people are located, they generally do not want to leave their homes. They know that Ebola patients who enter the hospital usually die. As a result, they think of the hospital as a place of death, not as a place to get better.

The problem is compounded in rural areas, where people are often superstitious and poorly educated. Sometimes the locals believe that angry spirits or other supernatural beings are making people sick. To these people, doctors, with their nonsense talk of germs, seem misinformed and foolish. Ebola patients and their families therefore feel no need to follow any medical advice they receive. Even worse, they sometimes believe that doctors or other authorities are actually responsible for the outbreak, and conflict may erupt as a result. In 2003, for instance, Congolese villagers thought that four local

When containment officials try to locate Ebola victims in rural communities like this one— in which people can be superstitious and uneducated—they are often regarded with suspicion.

schoolteachers had summoned Ebola through witchcraft. The teachers were stoned to death in an effort to halt the epidemic.

The Congo incident, luckily, was not typical. Containment teams can usually persuade Ebola victims to come to the hospital, where they will receive around-the-clock attention and care. Team members also convince family members, medical professionals, and others who have been exposed to Ebola to undergo regular health checks. These people must have their temperatures taken twice per day throughout Ebola's three-week incubation period. At the first sign of fever, they are hospitalized under strict isolation. Doctors will watch the patients carefully to see if they develop additional Ebola symptoms.

Community Education

No matter how hard a containment team tries, it will never find and isolate every Ebola case during an epidemic. For this reason, community education is an essential part of the outbreak management effort. People must know how to recognize Ebola, and they must know what to do if it occurs.

To spread the word about Ebola, officials assemble a team of local volunteers. The volunteers travel through the community and speak at schools, churches, marketplaces, restaurants, and other public places. They explain the disease's

A WHO official oversees the distribution of information about Ebola to residents of Kikwit. Education is key in preventing outbreaks.

Reactions to Ebola

During an Ebola outbreak, suspected victims are often shunned by the people around them. This was the experience of British reporter Pascale Harter, who became ill while covering an Ebola outbreak in Congo. Although Harter had malaria, not Ebola, the people around her were still terrified. In a 2003 article, Harter describes the reactions she noticed during her treatment.

The first doctor to visit me hesitated for ages outside the door, and I could see his colleagues edging away.

Eventually, he came in, sweat gathering behind his goggles, his gloved hands shaking. My examination lasted less than three minutes and the doctor was out of the door, taking off his protective suit to be burned. For eight days, no one would come near me. The British consulate brought me food and water but they had to leave it on the step for me to pick up. They couldn't hand anything to me in case our hands brushed and they couldn't accept anything from me. . . .

As I felt better . . . I amused myself by venturing to the door of my isolation unit and resting one foot on the step. This was my boundary, so at the first sign that I might cross it, the soldiers

symptoms and encourage people to contact the Ebola team within twenty-four hours if they notice these symptoms among their friends or family members. They also explain why people should avoid direct contact with sick or dead individuals. In short, they echo the information provided by the medical teams. Because the advice comes from community members, however, it is much more likely to be accepted and followed.

In addition to speaking, volunteers also pass out pamphlets written in the local language. The pamphlets answer basic questions about Ebola and try to dispel misconceptions. Because these materials are produced for specific populations and epidemics, they can also address matters of local concern. For instance, during a 2004 outbreak in Sudan, people were

[who were guarding the door] fell silent and their rifles began to twitch in their hands.

Pascale Harter, "My Ebola Horror in Congo," *Times* (London), June 18, 2003.

This woman was shunned by her community after she survived an Ebola infection.

afraid that they would never see their family members again if they sent them to the hospital. To respond to this fear, explains one account of the outbreak, officials "included pictures of the [isolation] ward in the pamphlet to show the local population that the fence around the ward was short enough for patients to see over and would allow them to talk to their family and friends from a safe distance."[30] These pictures reassured the community and made it less frightening for Ebola patients to seek help.

Like pamphlets, posters may also be reassuring during an epidemic. Local artists produce these materials, which are hung in public places throughout the epidemic area. The posters alert the public to the outbreak and explain how to stay healthy. They also tell people how to contact the Ebola team if they need help. By clearly explaining the situation, these materials reduce fear and make it easier for disease victims to cooperate with authorities.

Safe Burial

Even the most cooperative community, of course, cannot stop people from dying after they contract Ebola. During a severe outbreak, death may strike dozens of times a day, leaving piles of corpses behind. These corpses ooze virus for several days after death, so they can easily infect family members or anyone else who handles them.

Because corpses are so infectious, handling them properly and safely is a key task in any Ebola containment effort. But

In Gabon, a young Ebola victim is carried to her grave. Following arguments over local Gabonese burial customs, WHO found it prudent to evacuate its team members.

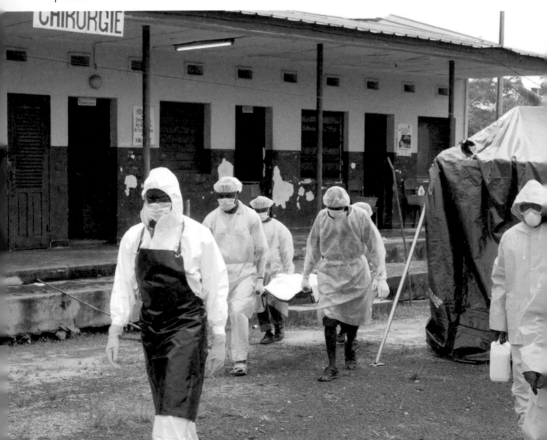

this job is not as straightforward as it seems. Containment teams nearly always meet resistance from family members who wish to handle the body. According to custom in many parts of Africa, corpses must be cleaned from head to toe, and they must spend several days with their families before burial. In some communities it is even traditional for wives or husbands to sleep with their dead spouses. Later, the corpses are often buried in shallow graves right next to people's homes. These activities can and often do spread Ebola to the deceased's friends and family.

To discourage unsafe burial practices, containment teams explain the dangers of these actions. They also organize funerals that are safe for everyone. These funerals, however, are grim affairs that involve protective gear for attendees, plastic-wrapped bodies, community graves, and the copious spraying of bleach to disinfect the area. Family members sometimes refuse to cooperate. If a family insists on a traditional burial despite the danger, says a WHO spokesman, "We are trying to tell [them] how to do so at the lowest possible risk. But it's really a tough fight."[31]

A situation that occurred during a 2001 Gabon outbreak illustrates just how tough the fight can be. During the containment effort, arguments over burial practices got so heated that members of the international team feared for their personal safety. WHO evacuated the team members temporarily to keep them from being hurt or killed by angry locals.

Although the 2001 situation was unusual, confrontations with upset family members over burial issues are not. These confrontations are very discouraging to containment teams. But no matter how unpleasant things get, teams continue to fight for the safe disposal of Ebola-ridden remains. It is their job to stop the epidemic, and handling corpses properly is an essential part of that task.

The Epidemic Winds Down

When safe burial and other containment efforts are used consistently, they eventually have the desired effect. The Ebola virus cannot find a way to spread from one person to another,

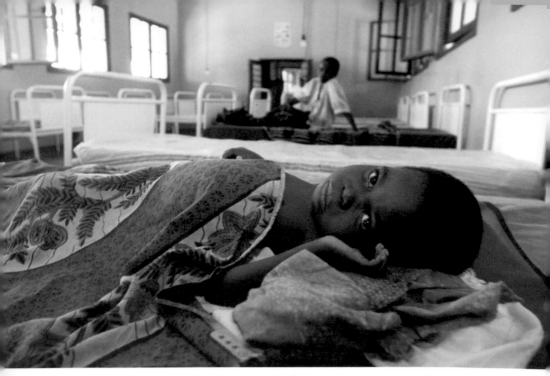

When formerly crowded isolation wards begin to empty, it may be a sign that an Ebola outbreak is on the wane.

and the epidemic starts to die down. This trend is most evident in hospitals, where formerly jammed isolation wards begin to empty out. Doctors cross their fingers as fewer and fewer patients arrive to replace those who have died or recovered. At some point, an entire day goes by with no new cases. The day may stretch into two, then three, then a week. It becomes clear that the outbreak is finally waning.

During this period the containment team shifts its focus from crisis management to data management as team members rush to gather information. They identify the index case and try to figure out exactly how he or she got sick. If possible, they visit the index case's work and home and collect a sampling of any creatures they find there. They take blood samples from patients who are still sick, and they take tissue specimens from corpses. They also collect blood and serum from people who recovered from Ebola. These survivor samples are especially precious. By studying them, scientists hope to discover exactly how some people fight off the deadly virus.

While team members collect information, they continue to monitor the community for signs of Ebola. Officials are fairly sure the epidemic is over once three weeks have passed with no new cases. However, the team continues to watch and wait for another three weeks, just to be safe. When no new cases have appeared for forty-two days—twice the longest-known incubation period for Ebola hemorrhagic fever—the outbreak is officially declared to be over.

Out of Africa

In African nations, Ebola presents unique challenges that must be handled in special ways. If the disease broke out in an industrial country, the problems and responses would be different. But at this point, no one knows exactly what these problems and responses might be. Except for the 1989 Reston incident, which did not affect humans, Ebola has never reached the general population in the Western world.

A few isolated cases of Ebola, however, have occurred outside Africa as the result of lab accidents. The handling of these cases has been very aggressive. Patients have been placed in much stricter isolation than anything possible in the African health-care setting, with all visitors forbidden. They have received constant nursing care along with carefully balanced fluids to combat dehydration. They have also received blood plasma from recovered Ebola victims as well as other experimental treatments. The results of these efforts have been encouraging. Of the four Ebola patients treated in the West, only one has died.

This statistic suggests that medical efforts in modern, well-equipped hospitals might really help Ebola patients during a Western-world epidemic. This would be a big improvement over the situation in rural Africa. Proper disposal of dead Ebola victims would also be easier in the West, where people tend to be less adamant about burial customs. Enforcing a quarantine, on the other hand, would undoubtedly be just as challenging. Viruses are relentless; their only purpose is to spread. Determined humans can stop this process, but containment efforts are always difficult and dangerous, no matter where Ebola may appear.

CHAPTER FIVE

Staying One Step Ahead

In the world of infectious disease, Ebola hemorrhagic fever is unusually grisly and deadly. These qualities have captured the attention of scientists, journalists, and the general public. As a result, Ebola receives a great deal of publicity whenever it appears.

Because Ebola gets so much attention, it is easy to forget that it has had very little effect on the human world. Since 1976, when Ebola was first recognized, the disease has been confirmed in fewer than two thousand people. Its impact is minuscule compared to that of AIDS, measles, yellow fever, and even the common flu, all of which are viral illnesses. Nonetheless, Ebola is a constant worry for health officials. Because the disease has no known cure, and because it kills such a high percentage of its victims, a major outbreak could devastate the human population. "[This is] the kind of fevered dream that wakes us up in a cold sweat,"[32] frets virologist C.J. Peters.

This dream, unfortunately, has a real chance of coming true. Viruses tend to spread from their home areas over time, and it is entirely possible that Ebola will do the same. To prepare for this eventuality, virologists around the world are searching for weapons that may help them during future Ebola epidemics.

Mapping Ebola

One of the most important steps in understanding Ebola is finding where it goes between outbreaks. Scientists feel certain that the virus lives naturally and harmlessly inside another living creature. According to virologist John Mills of the Centers for Disease Control and Prevention, locating this creature would be helpful in many ways:

> Once we identify the host of Ebola virus and learn its geographic range, habitat preferences, population dynamics and the cycle of infection in the host, we can then determine important things like the potential endemic area of the disease, which habitats and environments represent the greatest risk to humans, what times of the year provide increases in risk, and perhaps even how to predict specific times and places where increases in risk will occur.[33]

Despite decades of searching, however, no one has been able to pinpoint Ebola's natural reservoir. Scientists have unsuccessfully analyzed countless insects, spiders, reptiles, mammals, and even plants for signs of the virus. In 2005 one study did find evidence of Ebola in healthy fruit bats, which

Although a 2005 study found Ebola in healthy fruit bats like this one, scientists could not conclude with any certainty that the species is Ebola's natural reservoir.

suggests that these creatures might be the virus's natural carriers. But the results of this study are not conclusive. Many questions remain, and the search for the reservoir continues.

This job, unfortunately, is dauntingly large. Researchers might test thousands of creatures without finding a single Ebola carrier. They might even examine an uninfected member of Ebola's reservoir, in which case the connection would be missed. As one scientist explains, "You can test 100,000 mosquitoes for a certain virus until you find it; that's the sort of job we face."[34]

To narrow the hunt, one team of virologists has analyzed the geography of Ebola. In 2003 the team recorded the precise location of every known Ebola index case. It then used U.S. Geological Survey databases to find climate information for each of these locations, including average temperature, rainfall, solar radiation, and more. This information was plugged into a computer program that identified other areas with similar conditions. The study's authors believe that Ebola's reservoir will be found in these places, and they suggest that all other areas should be excluded from consideration. Doing so, they say, could make the search process much easier and lead to faster answers.

Human Habits

Scientists do not know exactly which creature harbors Ebola. They are fairly sure, however, that the animal in question lives in the densest parts of the rain forest. This unknown carrier has probably been passing Ebola to monkeys and other creatures for hundreds of years. These creatures, in turn, were almost certainly infecting humans long before Ebola's official discovery. Occasional mysterious deaths would not have been questioned in rural Africa, where infectious diseases kill an estimated 5 million people per year.

Ebola might have remained a hit-and-run killer, picking off the occasional person but otherwise staying hidden, if humans in Africa had not changed their ways of living. One major change occurred in the mid-1900s, when growing populations started expanding into formerly untouched regions. Another

Scientists speculate that the primary host for Ebola is a creature living in the darkest reaches of rain forests like this one in Gabon.

change has involved the increasing industrialization of Africa. Today, logging operations and other commercial efforts bring people into the continent's most remote regions. By entering virgin rain forests, these people increase their risk of encountering Ebola. As one scientist points out, "Everybody in the West loves the idea of biodiversity in rainforests. Well, people forget that that includes microbes, too. Look at it from the perspective of these viruses. Look who's invading [whom]."[35]

Invading viruses would not be a problem, of course, if sick people stayed in the rain forest and had no contact with the outside world. But in modern times, there are numerous ways for Ebola to spread beyond its point of origin. Diseased villagers might travel to major hospitals, where they could pass Ebola to other patients and thus to the community at large. Infected loggers might climb into their vehicles at the end of the workday and head toward local cities, where they could sicken people in bars, restaurants, and other public places. Ebola-

Screeners at airports should be trained to watch for obviously ill passengers as part of the effort to stop Ebola from spreading throughout the world.

ridden truckers might deliver products to distant areas, possibly spreading disease as they go. Boats, trains, and airplanes are other likely vectors for the transport of Ebola.

So far, the Ebola virus has not managed to take advantage of these possibilities. But scientists do not believe humankind can stay lucky forever. They fear that Ebola will eventually break out of the rain forest and strike Africa's large cities, where sanitation and health care are substandard at best. If this happens, says one virologist, "We can expect a lot more trouble."[36]

Ebola Goes International

Even more frightening than a major African outbreak is the prospect that Ebola may spread internationally. History shows that tropical diseases often make their way to other areas. Lassa fever, for instance, is endemic to central Africa but pops up frequently among international travelers. Another disease called West Nile fever was originally found in Uganda but now affects parts of North America and Europe as well. There is no reason Ebola might not make the same leap someday. As scientist David Heymann of the World Health Organization says, "We can't rely on our little space suits to insulate us from Africa anymore. With trade, travel, global investments, it just ain't that kind of world any longer."[37]

If Ebola did hop continents, it would probably do it via airplane. Today, air travel makes it possible for people to reach any major city in the world within twenty-four hours. An infected person could easily carry Ebola from Africa to North America, Europe, Asia, Australia, or any other region before developing symptoms. The person might make other travelers sick along the way, and he or she might infect friends, family members, and other contacts soon after arrival. In a major city like New York, where crowded conditions are typical, an epidemic could become uncontrollable before health authorities realized they had a problem.

In 2001 an Ebola scare showed just how easy it would be for an infected person to reach the Western world. In early February of that year, a woman traveled from the Democratic Republic of the Congo to Canada. She made stops along the way at the bustling international airports in Rome, Italy, and Newark, New Jersey. When the woman finally reached Toronto, Canada, she left the airport without attracting any particular attention. Three days later, however, she was rushed to the hospital with symptoms that resembled Ebola. Doctors immediately isolated the patient and sent blood samples to a laboratory for testing. A day later they breathed a sigh of relief when they received the lab report: no Ebola.

In the aftermath of this incident, Canadian health officials praised the hospital for its textbook handling of the situation. But they also sounded a somber note in regard to airport screening. "There are techniques available to screen every passenger coming off a flight, but it is extremely expensive and the return would be close to zero,"[38] explains David Groves, president of the Canadian Association for Clinical Microbiology and Infectious Diseases. In other words, it simply is not practical to examine every airline passenger for Ebola and other tropical diseases.

Airport screeners can, however, be trained to watch for obviously ill travelers. They are particularly careful when a flight arrives from an area where Ebola and other viral hemorrhagic fevers are endemic. If a passenger looks unwell, he or she may be taken aside and examined. Unfortunately, Ebola victims who feel well enough to travel probably do not have any symptoms yet, so airport screening is an extremely flimsy defense against the disease.

Could Ebola Evolve?

There is a reassuring side, however, to the air-travel issue. Because the Ebola virus spreads through direct contact with bodily fluids, a carrier with no symptoms is very unlikely to make other people sick. This is true even in a cramped airplane cabin, where people spend long hours together in very close quarters. Within Africa, in fact, several known Ebola carriers have traveled by airplane without infecting other passengers.

But virologists are still concerned. They call attention to the fact that viruses change over time. As C.J. Peters explains, "RNA-based viruses tend to be not terribly careful or accurate

Even though airline passengers occupy tight quarters, an Ebola carrier with no symptoms is unlikely to infect others on the flight.

replicators, compared with their DNA cousins. Each time an influenza virus enters a host, for example, what comes back out can be slightly different from the strain that went in. You do this enough times . . . and you can end up with something substantially different."[39]

In Ebola's case, scientists worry that the virus may change in ways that allow it to travel through the air. They point out that one strain, Ebola-Reston, has already developed this ability. If deadlier strains did the same, the result would be devastating. Philip Russell, an Army general who was involved in the 1989 Reston incident, vividly recalls the moment he first faced this possibility:

> When I saw the respiratory evidence coming from those [Reston] monkeys, I said to myself, My God, with certain kinds of small changes, this virus could become one that travels in rapid respiratory transmission through humans. I'm talking about the Black Death. Imagine a virus with the infectiousness of influenza and the mortality rate of the black plague in the Middle Ages—that's what we're talking about.[40]

The AIDS Highway

The Kinshasa Highway is an east-west roadway that cuts through the heart of Africa. Paved during the 1970s, this highway allowed AIDS to escape from remote African villages and reach the world at large. It is a prime example of the way human activities affect emerging viruses.

In a 1999 article entitled "The Emergence of AIDS: Kinshasa Highway," author Catherine Howard explains the road's history and significance.

[The Kinshasa Highway] was once a wandering dirt track, practically impossible to travel along. In the 1970s it was paved and soon after boasted a heavy traffic flow. This encouraged the movement of natives out of their villages and into the big cities. The problem was that many of them were also carrying AIDS.

To cater to the travelers, particularly truck drivers, along the highway, small restaurants sprang up along its length. Some of these establishments also provided a bed for the night and others provided extras that discreetly went unadvertised. Doctors believe that 90% of all prostitutes working along the main African roads are infected with the AIDS virus. . . .

Kinshasa Highway is the road that boasts the world's highest death toll, yet none of its victims have died on the road. They have perished at the hands of a lethal microscopic virus. [By 1999], conservative estimates [held] AIDS responsible for the loss of ten million lives.

Catherine Howard, "The Emergence of AIDS: Kinshasa Highway," *Student Xpress*, March 1999. www.studentxpress.ie/student/VOL1/ISSUE1/The%20Emergence%20of%20Aids.htm.

Scientists disagree about the likelihood of this scenario. Some even dismiss it entirely. "There's no reason to think that a virus normally transmitted only through body fluids would suddenly mutate and start traveling by air. In any case, even if it did become airborne, Ebola wouldn't survive more than a few minutes in the atmosphere; ultraviolet light destroys it,"[41] says one writer. In this person's opinion, Ebola is and will remain poorly equipped to mount a global attack.

Other people, however, are slower to discount an airborne Ebola crisis. They observe that the more time Ebola spends in human hosts, the more likely it is to develop new and possibly deadly traits, Furthermore, because viruses multiply and change very quickly, these traits could appear with little or no warning. In a worst-case situation, airborne Ebola might emerge, spread, and turn a bustling city into a morgue within several weeks.

Ebola as a Weapon

Airborne Ebola might not occur naturally. In a 1995 study, however, scientists at the U.S. Army Medical Research Institute of Infectious Diseases proved that the virus can travel through the air if it is added to a very fine aerosol. The authors of this study exposed monkeys to water vapor laden with Ebola-Zaire. All of the monkeys developed Ebola hemorrhagic fever and died within four to five days.

This study has some alarming implications. In particular, it suggests that Ebola could be used as a biological weapon. Author Pete Moore explains how easy it would be for terrorists to spread the virus:

> All a terror campaign needs is some method of generating an aerosol, and there are plenty of low-tech systems to choose from. An agricultural crop sprayer would be one way to discharge massive doses. . . . Pressurized aerosol cans will do a great job, and the backpack sprayers that you can pick up at any garden equipment store will be okay.[42]

Using any of these items, terrorists could spread a lethal fog of Ebola in a subway or another crowded place.

Distributing the Ebola virus might be simple, but obtaining it, fortunately, is not. It would be very difficult for a terrorist organization to find a suitable supply. And even if a terror group did somehow acquire a stock of Ebola, the virus might very well kill its handlers before it could be released. Still, this prospect does not discourage determined terrorists. Adherents of Japan's Aum Shinrikyo (or Aleph) religion, for instance, visited Zaire during one Ebola outbreak with the stated goal of providing medical assistance. But because this sect is known for developing and using biological weapons, officials strongly suspect that the Aum Shinrikyo members were actually trying to gather raw Ebola.

No one knows whether the sect succeeded in its mission, but one thing is certain: If the terrorists did acquire Ebola, they have not yet released it. The virus has never been used in a deliberate attack. This does not mean, however, that such an attack could not occur in the future. In an age of increased terrorism, Ebola is a potentially deadly weapon that cannot be ignored.

The Search for a Vaccine

This possibility would be much less worrisome if doctors had drugs that could fight Ebola. Researchers are therefore working to find or develop substances that might have an effect on the disease.

The most promising area of study right now involves a potential Ebola vaccine. In a 2005 paper, American and Canadian virologists explained that they had changed a harmless virus to make it resemble Ebola. This altered virus—still harmless—was injected into four monkeys; two other control monkeys did not receive the drug. A few weeks later, all six monkeys received lethal doses of Ebola virus. The control monkeys immediately developed Ebola hemorrhagic fever and died, as expected, but the other four monkeys stayed perfectly healthy. The vaccine had "taught" their bodies how to destroy Ebola before the actual virus ever appeared.

Not only did the vaccine work, but it was also easy to use. Some vaccines need to be given several times before they produce immunity, but the Ebola vaccine did it with a single injection. "You need to go in and vaccinate the population in a very short period of time . . . so that's a major breakthrough,"[43] explains Tom Geisbert, the principal author of the study.

No one knows yet if this monkey vaccine will protect people from Ebola, but scientists are hopeful. Monkeys and humans react in almost identical ways to the virus, which suggests that they might react in identical ways to the vaccine as well. "The fact that [the vaccine] so robustly protected monkeys, which are a good model for this disease . . . can't be guaranteed, but [we have] optimism that it'll work in a human,"[44] says one leading virologist.

Although the Ebola vaccine is promising, testing it on human subjects is a tricky proposition. Researchers have injected the vaccine into volunteers to prove it is safe, but they have no idea whether these volunteers are now immune to Ebola. To answer this question, they would need to expose the

A Cure for Ebola?

So far, scientists have not discovered any way to cure Ebola in humans. But one treatment does show promise in laboratory monkeys. In 2003 researchers injected twelve test subjects with Ebola-Zaire—usually 100 percent fatal in monkeys. Nine of the monkeys then received daily doses of a protein that blocks clotting. Scientists hoped that this protein would stop the monkeys' circulatory systems from getting clogged with blood clots. This would take stress off the body and give the monkeys time to develop an immune response.

The results of the test supported this theory. The control group of three untreated monkeys developed classic Ebola symptoms and died quickly. Out of the nine treated monkeys, however, three survived—a success rate of 33 percent. In the others, the disease took about four days longer than usual to run its course. This is a hopeful finding because, as virologist C.J. Peters explains, "What we're doing with Ebola is we're buying time. The difference between Ebola and AIDS is that with Ebola, you do have the possibility of an immune response and to get well—if you can hang around long enough."

Quoted in Emma Ross, "Progress in Treating Ebola Reported," MSNBC.com, December 12, 2003. www.msnbc.msn.com/id/9093046.

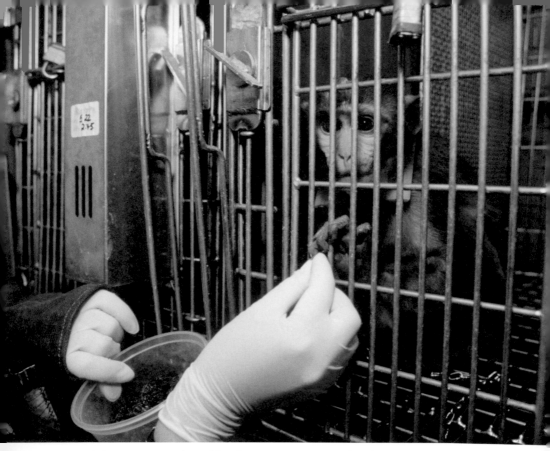

Using laboratory monkeys like this one, scientists developed a vaccine that effectively protects monkeys from the Ebola virus.

test subjects to the virus. Doing this would be unethical and dangerous, not to mention illegal, so this type of experiment will never be carried out under laboratory conditions. The vaccine could, however, be tested in the field during a real-life Ebola outbreak. When people are being exposed to the virus anyway, there is nothing wrong with giving them an experimental drug that might do some good.

Protecting the Masses

If tests show that the Ebola vaccine does work in humans, the virus will become much less frightening to world health officials. Researchers, doctors, nurses, and anyone else who has regular contact with Ebola would be safe from the virus. The family members and friends of known Ebola patients could be vaccinated so they would not get sick. Even the patients themselves might benefit. In laboratory tests, sick monkeys that received the vaccine lived several days longer than untreated monkeys. If the vaccine has the same effect in humans, it might keep a patient alive long enough to fight the virus on his or her own. For all these reasons, an Ebola vaccine would be incredibly useful during an outbreak.

It might seem that a vaccine could even stop Ebola from appearing at all. Everyone living in Sudan, the Democratic Republic of Congo (DRC), and other endemic Ebola areas could be vaccinated as a general precaution. Unfortunately, this is not likely to happen. Ebola is so rare that it does not make sense to vaccinate every possible potential victim. Also, a widespread vaccination program would be too expensive for the countries that need it most. As one doctor in the DRC says, "To maintain hygiene, you need funds, and we don't have them."[45] Hospitals that struggle to afford basic necessities certainly cannot give out millions of free Ebola vaccinations.

Because widespread vaccination is impractical, Ebola hemorrhagic fever will be a continuing problem in Africa even if a vaccine exists. A vaccine also cannot stop Ebola from traveling to developed countries or being used as a biological weapon. If these situations do arise, however, a vaccine would give containment teams at least one good weapon against the virus. It would also make any containment effort much safer for scientists and medical professionals, all of whom could be protected against Ebola.

Further Study Is Needed

Besides working on a vaccine, researchers are studying many other aspects of Ebola. They are trying to learn how the virus behaves during an infection and the exact effects it has on the human body. They are looking for ways to treat Ebola. They are also continuing to hunt for Ebola's reservoir. All of these efforts, however, are proceeding slowly. Ebola occurs in remote areas and emerges only occasionally, so it is very hard to study in the field. Also, scientists have trouble raising money to pay for Ebola research when other diseases, such as AIDS, are considered so much more pressing. As long as Ebola remains a rare African disease, it probably will not get much attention.

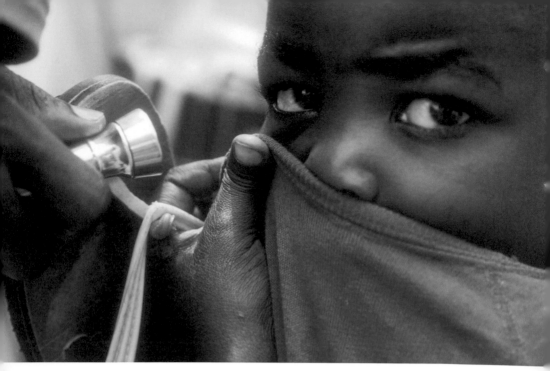

A boy covers his face as a defense against the Ebola virus. Long-term financial support for Ebola research is eclipsed by funding for AIDS.

Daniel Bausch, a scientist with the CDC's Special Pathogens Branch, thinks this approach is a mistake. In a 2001 United Nations publication, Bausch explained his view on the matter:

> Short-term financial commitments for a high-profile outbreak are relatively easily forthcoming, but long-term support . . . is scarce. This is unfortunate, as long-term investigations . . . would ultimately have far more of an impact on health than the measure of our emergency response to any single given outbreak. The point is not that one is more important than the other, but rather that if there was more of the former, there would be a lot less need for the latter.[46]

Many virologists agree with Bausch. They believe preparation is the key to controlling Ebola, so they will keep studying the virus as best they can. Without financial support, however, there is only so much these scientists can do. Until Ebola becomes a problem for nations that can afford to fund research efforts, the virus is likely to remain a poorly understood but deadly curiosity.

Notes

Chapter 1: Death in Africa

1. Joseph B. McCormick and Susan Fisher-Hoch, *Level 4: Virus Hunters of the CDC*. Atlanta: Turner, 1996, p. 53.
2. Frank Ryan, *Virus X: Tracking the New Killer Plagues*. Boston: Little, Brown, 1997, pp. 153–154.
3. Quoted in Ryan, *Virus X*, p. 170.
4. Quoted in Richard Preston, *The Hot Zone*. New York: Random House, 1994, p. 83.
5. Quoted in Ryan, *Virus X*, p. 187.
6. McCormick and Fisher-Hoch, *Level 4*, p. 44.

Chapter 2: The Science of Ebola

7. Preston, *The Hot Zone*, p. 26.
8. Preston, *The Hot Zone*, p. 81.
9. McCormick and Fisher-Hoch, *Level 4*, p. 17.
10. Preston, *The Hot Zone*, p. 20.
11. Preston, *The Hot Zone*, p. 13.
12. Charles Wendo, "Caring for the Survivors of Uganda's Ebola Epidemic One Year On," *Lancet*, October 20, 2001, p. 1350.
13. Ryan, *Virus X*, p. 236.
14. Ryan, *Virus X*, p. 236.

Chapter 3: Ebola Reappears

15. Roy C. Baron, Joseph B. McCormick, and Osman A. Zubeir, "Ebola Virus Disease in Southern Sudan: Hospital Dissemination and Intrafamilial Spread," *Bulletin of the World Health Organization*, vol. 61, no. 6, 1983, p. 1001.
16. C.J. Peters and Mark Olshaker, *Virus Hunter: Thirty Years of Battling Hot Viruses Around the World*. New York: Anchor, 1997, p. 3.
17. Peters and Olshaker, *Virus Hunter*, p. 6.

18. Peters and Olshaker, *Virus Hunter*, p. 271.
19. Quoted in Nancy Gibbs and Andrew Purvis, "In Search of the Dying," *Time*, May 29, 1995.
20. David L. Heymann et al., "Ebola Hemorrhagic Fever: Lessons from Kikwit, Democratic Republic of the Congo," *Journal of Infectious Diseases*, Volume 179, supplement 1, February 1999, p. 283.
21. Heymann et al., "Ebola Hemorrhagic Fever," p. 284.
22. Heymann et al., "Ebola Hemorrhagic Fever," p. 284.

Chapter 4: Containing Ebola
23. Baron, McCormick, and Zubeir, "Ebola Virus Disease in Southern Sudan," p. 1001.
24. World Health Organization, "Epidemic Intelligence— Systematic Event Detection." www.who.int/csr/alert response/epidemicintelligence/en/index.html.
25. World Health Organization, "Global Outbreak Alert and Response Network—Partnership in Outbreak Response." www.who.int/csr/outbreaknetwork/goarnenglish.pdf.
26. Laurie Garrett, *The Coming Plague: Newly Emerging Diseases in a World Out of Balance*. New York: Farrar, Straus and Giroux, 1994, p. 220.
27. Centers for Disease Control Special Pathogens Branch, "Infection Control for Viral Haemorrhagic Fevers in the African Health Care Setting." www.cdc.gov/ncidod/dvrd/spb/mnpages/vhfmanual/section3.htm.
28. McCormick and Fisher-Hoch, *Level 4*, p. 49.
29. Quoted in Gibbs and Purvis, "In Search of the Dying."
30. *Weekly Epidemiological Record*, "Outbreak of Ebola Haemorrhagic Fever in Yambio, South Sudan, April–June 2004," October 28, 2005, p. 372.
31. Quoted in Gibbs and Purvis, "In Search of the Dying."

Chapter 5: Staying One Step Ahead
32. Peters and Olshaker, *Virus Hunter*, p. 1.
33. Quoted in Karen Palmer, "Trio Maps Behavior of Elusive Ebola Virus," *Toronto Star*, April 11, 2003, p. D2.
34. Quoted in Paul Salopek, "Nothing Shapes Character

of Life in Africa More than Deadly Illness, Including Ebola," *Chicago Tribune*, January 7, 2000.

35. Quoted in Salopek, "Nothing Shapes Character of Life in Africa More than Deadly Illness, Including Ebola."

36. Quoted in Geoffrey Cowley and Joseph Contreras, "Outbreak of Fear," *Newsweek*, May 22, 1995.

37. Quoted in Salopek, "Nothing Shapes Character of Life in Africa More than Deadly Illness, Including Ebola."

38. Quoted in Clare O'Hara, "Ebola Scare Turns Out to Be a False Alarm," *University of Western Ontario Gazette*, February 8, 2001.

39. Peters and Olshaker, *Virus Hunter*, pp. 238–39.

40. Quoted in Preston, *The Hot Zone*, p. 254.

41. Quoted in Cowley and Contreras, "Outbreak of Fear."

42. Pete Moore, *Killer Germs: Rogue Diseases of the Twenty-First Century*. London: Carlton, 2001, p. 199.

43. Quoted in Ernest Leong, "Development of New Ebola Vaccine Considered Major Breakthrough," VOANews.com, June 10, 2005. www.voanews.com/english/archive/2005-06/2005-06-10-voa53.cfm.

44. *Talk of the Nation*, "Interview: Dr. Anthony Fauci Discusses Progress on Ebola Vaccine," August 8, 2003.

45. Quoted in Gibbs and Purvis, "In Search of the Dying."

46. Daniel Bausch, "The Ebola Virus and the Challenges to Health Research in Africa," *U.N. Chronicle*, no. 2, 2001, p. 10.

Glossary

antibiotic: A substance that is able to kill bacteria.

antibody: A protein that is produced by the body when viruses or other foreign material are detected. This protein binds to and neutralizes the foreign materials.

biodiversity: The number and variety of organisms found within a region.

blood serum: A watery part of the blood that resembles plasma but contains clotting substances.

contagious: Able to be transmitted by direct or indirect contact.

contaminated: Infected by contact with an unclean material.

control: In vaccination experiments, a control is a test subject that does not receive the experimental drug but is treated exactly the same in all other ways as the subjects that do receive the drug.

convalescence: The recovery period that follows an illness.

emerging disease: An infectious disease that has newly appeared in a population or that has been known for some time but is rapidly increasing in incidence or geographic range.

endemic: Native to a particular region.

epidemic: An outbreak that strikes a large number of people in a certain area during the same period.

euthanize: To deliberately cause death in a merciful and virtually painless way.

filovirus: A threadlike virus of the family Filoviridae. Ebola and Marburg are the only known filoviruses.

hemorrhagic: Characterized by heavy or uncontrollable bleeding.

incubation period: The time between exposure to a virus and development of noticeable symptoms.

index case: The earliest documented case of a disease in a specific outbreak.

infectious disease: A disease that is caused by a biological agent, such as a virus, rather than physical or genetic factors.

inoculation: The introduction of a pathogen into an organism to encourage the development of antibodies.

interferon: A protein that prevents some viruses from replicating.

microbe: A very small organism, particularly one that causes disease.

natural reservoir: The long-term host of a virus that causes an infectious disease.

nosocomial transmission: The transmission of an infectious disease in a hospital setting.

outbreak: A sudden eruption of disease in a population.

pathogen: An agent that causes disease.

pathology: The scientific study of the nature of disease and its causes, processes, development, and consequences.

quarantine: The isolation of actual or suspected disease victims, designed to prevent the spread of the illness.

replication: The process by which genetic material or a virus copies itself.

ribavirin: A drug that slows down the replication of some viruses.

ribonucleic acid (RNA): In viruses, a molecule that contains all of the microbe's genetic information.

vaccine: A harmless substance that stimulates an immune response to a specific disease when introduced into a person's body.

vector: An organism, vehicle, or any other means of transportation that carries disease-causing microorganisms from one host to another.

viral: Relating to viruses.

viral hemorrhagic fever (VHF): A viral illness characterized by fever, gastrointestinal symptoms, and bleeding.

virion: A single, complete virus particle.

virologist: A scientist who specializes in the study of viruses.

virus: A microbe consisting of genetic material surrounded by a protein coat. It requires living cells for replication and often causes disease in host organisms.

Organizations to Contact

Centers for Disease Control and Prevention (CDC)
1600 Clifton Rd., Atlanta, GA 30333
(404) 639-3311
www.cdc.gov

The CDC is one of the thirteen major operating components of the U.S. Department of Health and Human Services. As one of the world's top research labs, it plays a major role in researching and taking action against Ebola hemorrhagic fever and other emerging diseases.

U.S. Army Medical Research Institute for Infectious Diseases (USAMRIID)
1425 Porter St., Frederick, MD 21702-5111
www.usamriid.army.mil

Located in Maryland's Fort Detrick, USAMRIID is the U.S. military's top scientific laboratory. USAMRIID scientists conduct basic and applied research on Ebola and other biological threats. The organization's purpose is to develop medical solutions for the protection of military service members.

World Health Organization (WHO)
Avenue Appia 20 1211, Geneva 27, Switzerland
www.who.int

A part of the United Nations, WHO works to help people achieve physical, mental, and social well-being. WHO's Web site contains current information on diseases affecting people all over the world.

For Further Reading

Books

William T. Close, *Ebola Through the Eyes of the People*. Marbleton, WY: Meadowlark Springs, 2002. This account of the 1976 Ebola epidemic in Yambuku was written by a doctor who spent many years working in Africa. Although the book is fictionalized, it is often cited as the most accurate existing reference on the subject.

Joseph B. McCormick and Susan Fisher-Hoch, *Level 4: Virus Hunters of the CDC*. Atlanta: Turner, 1996. In this book, world-renowned virologists McCormick and Fisher-Hoch describe their experiences hunting Ebola and other Level 4 viruses.

C.J. Peters and Mark Olshaker, *Virus Hunter: Thirty Years of Battling Hot Viruses Around the World*. New York: Anchor, 1997. One of the world's top virus hunters describes his role in humankind's ongoing battle against emerging diseases.

Richard Preston, *The Hot Zone*. New York: Random House, 1994. Subtitled *A Terrifying True Story*, this gripping book tells the tale of the 1989 Ebola outbreak in Reston, Virginia. It includes a great deal of background information on the Ebola and Marburg viruses as well.

Periodicals

Daniel Bausch, "The Ebola Virus and the Challenges to Health Research in Africa," *U.N. Chronicle*, no. 2, 2001. This article presents an excellent overview of some political obstacles that stand in the way of Ebola research.

Journal of Infectious Diseases, February 1999. Available online at www.journals.uchicago.edu/JID/journal/contents/v179nS1.html. The three-hundred-page issue, devoted entirely to scientific studies of Ebola, is posted online. The main bodies of some articles are written at a challenging level, but the introductions and conclusions are generally easy to read and contain a great deal of useful information.

Richard Preston, "The Bioweaponeers," *New Yorker*, March 9, 1998. This lengthy article takes a frightening look at Russia's biological weapons program. One weapon designed to deploy the Marburg virus is highlighted. Although the article is a bit dated, it is a well-written overview of biological warfare in general.

Web Sites

Centers for Disease Control and Prevention (www.cdc. gov). This is the official site of the CDC. Search for "Ebola" to uncover a wealth of information about the virus and the disease.

Weekly Epidemiological Record (www.who.int/wer/en/). This site provides electronic copies of the *Weekly Epidemiological Record*, the World Health Organization's weekly summary of world disease activity. An excellent source of as-it-happened information on every Ebola outbreak since the disease was discovered.

World Health Organization (www.who.int). Like the CDC Web site, the WHO Web site contains a great deal of information on Ebola and other emerging diseases.

Video

Nova, *Ebola: The Plague Fighters*, 1996. The Ebola virus and its devastating impact are profiled as camera operators travel behind the scenes during the 1995 Kikwit epidemic. Note that this documentary contains some graphic scenes of Ebola victims in the throes of the disease.

Index

Picture Credits

About the Author

Kris Hirschmann has written more than 130 books for children. She owns and runs The Wordshop (www.the-wordshop. com), a business that provides a variety of writing and editorial services. She holds a bachelor's degree in psychology from Dartmouth College in Hanover, New Hampshire. Hirschmann lives just outside Orlando, Florida, with her husband, Michael, and her daughters, Nikki and Erika.